The Way It Is

The Way It Is

by Curt Flood

with Richard Carter

TRIDENT PRESS   NEW YORK

796.357
F65w

74924
August, 1971

The material quoted on pp. 205–206
is copyright, ©, 1970, by The New York Times
Company. Reprinted by permission.

SBN: 671–27076–1
LIBRARY OF CONGRESS CATALOG CARD NUMBER: 70–143045

PUBLISHED SIMULTANEOUSLY IN THE UNITED STATES AND CANADA
BY TRIDENT PRESS, A DIVISION OF SIMON & SCHUSTER, INC.,
630 FIFTH AVENUE, NEW YORK, N.Y. 10020

PRINTED IN THE UNITED STATES OF AMERICA

To Marian Jorgensen, in loving memory of Johnny.

Pharaoh, you better let them chillun go, honey.

CARL FLOOD
February 1970

Contents

The Way It Is

1

The Butterflies of March

I awoke prudently, opening neither eye. The bed was un-
mistakably mine. This meant that St. Louis lay in
winter sorrow nineteen floors below. The marauding in-
evitabilities of time and place stormed through the outskirts
of my mind. I tried to reopen negotiations with sleep, but
it had gone.

If I chose, I could extend a hand, touch buttons and
engulf myself in the balanced clamor of eight loudspeakers,
obliterating the moment without restraining the clock or
calendar. Beyond my bedroom door a manila folder lurked,
pregnant with overdue portrait commissions. Canvas awaits
brush. Brush awaits mood. Mood waits.

That cracked it. Does the vodka martini induce disaster?
Or does disaster induce the vodka martini? It had been a
singular night. She behaved like a woman with a claim, as
if we had already explored deep secrets. Her possessive bab-
ble perplexed and irritated me, but she wanted to come
home. I tuned her out and brought her along. As we ap-

proached the entrance to the lobby she became strident. She charged that I had forgotten her name, face and previous visit. It must have been true. Then she rushed away, which may have been a waste. I wondered if something of the kind had not happened before. I could not remember.

I kicked off the covers and pronounced myself available to the day. Microscopic wings fluttered in my stomach. Anxiety's butterflies. Old companions lately returned, like the swallows of spring. I considered opening the bureau drawer and inspecting the clutter of commemorative watches and rings, the trinkets of prowess. I thought better of it. Picked my way to the bathroom mirror and permitted my bloody eyes to reproach themselves ever so gently. Then past Marian's room (dear Babe), and the lair of my absent brother and onward to the kitchen for the restorative beer. The windows were uncommonly bright, the apartment stuffy. Sunshine! I moved through the living room and pushed open the terrace door. I smelled spring's first mildness. The butterflies quickened.

I withdrew to a couch and consulted the beer. My body protested. It was not programmed for morning beer in a St. Louis apartment on a sunny March 2. Years of habit had established a seasonal craving for other pursuits and a different setting. To suspend discomfort, I had only to make a simple telephone call. Physiology upset? Emotions infirm? Use the telephone for fast, fast, fast relief. I fetched another beer. My legs needed to run, my arms to flail. Not a chance. No way. Forget it.

Larry Albert arrived punctually with the usual sheaf of letters from the Missouri Department of Health and Welfare:

"This is to inform you that a Miss A—— R——, living at 2516 —— Street in St. Louis, needs shoes for her daughters, ages 5, 14, 15, 16 and 18, and for her sons, ages 6,

10, 12 and 13. A letter has been written to Miss R——, informing her of your services. Any help you could give would be appreciated. Very truly yours . . ."

Having assigned themselves other commitments, the United States of America, the State of Missouri and the City of St. Louis could not in good conscience provide shoes for the children of the poor. Enter Larry Albert, founder and executive director of The Aunts and Uncles, Inc., which tries to come up with the shoes. I am the president of the little organization but Larry is the motivating force. We have given tens of thousands of pairs of shoes. We are very big on shoes. They sometimes make it bearable for a child to go to school, where he might begin to find the way to a satisfactory life. Moreover, the presentation of brand-new, well-fitted shoes without ritual, price or penance is a rare and illuminating experience for such a child. The gift suggests that someone cares, and that the child is worth it, and that the world contains possibilities other than wretchedness.

Leading citizens of St. Louis contrived years ago to obtain federal and municipal funds with which to beautify the Mississippi riverfront. At a cost which had approached $40 million and was still increasing in 1970, they caused the construction there of the Jefferson National Expansion Memorial. Its principal feature is the renowned Gateway Arch, undoubtedly the most stupendous ornament in North America. Of stainless steel with a concrete core, the sublime object soars above downtown St. Louis like a huge croquet wicket. It spans 630 feet of land. Its apex cleaves the sky at an altitude equal to the span—more than twice the height of the Statue of Liberty.

The wicket celebrates the city's geographic and historic good fortune as gateway to the West. It stands also as an emblem of local and national priorities. A scant few blocks

away are some of the most horrible slums in the United
States. And barely yards from the arch is the old court-
house in which Dred Scott sued for his freedom.

From the shattered windows of the worst of the slums—
the government-sponsored ghetto called Pruitt-Igoe—10,000
inheritors of old Dred's disappointment are free to enjoy
superb views of the arch and to draw what conclusions
they will. Their proximity to the city's glinting symbol of
unconcern was especially educational during the merciless
winter of 1969–70, when Pruitt-Igoe heating pipes burst,
ice mantled the floors and subzero temperatures punished
the residents for their helplessness.

After ample experience elsewhere, I can testify that St.
Louis is no more barbaric than other cities in the United
States. I mention children's shoes and the symbolism of
an arch only to supply context for recollections deeply felt.
As the reader may already know, the story itself is about
a career in professional baseball. Customary though it may
be to write about that institutionalized pastime as though
it existed apart from the general environment, my story
does not lend itself to such treatment. In fact, without
attention to its social setting, the story would be incompre-
hensible and so would I. This is not said apologetically.
The facts are that nobody who plays professional baseball
or owns its teams or reports its goings-on to the public is
exempt from what takes place beyond the stadium walls.
Some of the players hope that they are and most of the
more sedentary members of the cast pretend that they are,
but you will get no such mythology here.

I was on the St. Louis Cardinals for twelve years. With
the exception of one or two outstanding pitchers and home-
run hitters (I was neither), I became the most highly paid
performer in the history of the team. In October 1969, five
months before the day on which these reminiscences be-

gin, the Cardinals traded me and some other players to Philadelphia.

Player trades are commonplace. The unusual aspect of this one was that I refused to accept it. It violated the logic and integrity of my existence. I was not a consignment of goods. I was a man, the rightful proprietor of my own person and my own talents.

A salesman reluctant to transfer from one office to another may choose to seek employment on the sales force of a different firm. A plumber can reject the dictates of his boss without relinquishing his right to plumb elsewhere. At the expiration of one contract, an actor shops among producers for the best arrangement he can find. But the baseball monopoly offers no such option to the athlete. If he elects not to work for the corporation that "owns" his services, baseball forbids him to ply his trade at all. In the hierarchy of living things, he ranks with poultry.

The Philadelphia Phillies offered me $100,000 to play center field for them during the 1970 season. I did not earn that much from the struggling Curt Flood Photo Studios, or from painting portraits. One of the leading wags in the baseball establishment remarked that, unless Curt Flood were another Rembrandt, he'd show up in time to play for the Phillies and collect his pay. Members of that establishment, including its wags, were entirely incapable of understanding that a basic principle of human life was involved. More to the point, they recognized no principle so basic that it could not be nullified by payment of a few extra dollars.

I sued. The distinguished Mr. Justice Arthur J. Goldberg went to Federal Court in my behalf and challenged the right of entrepreneurs to use me for barter, like a chattel. Baseball had been sued on similar grounds in the past, but never by an Arthur Goldberg and never by a player with my credentials, my resources or my particular brand of rage.

To challenge the sanctity of organized baseball was to question one of the primary myths of the American culture. To persist in the heresy required profound conviction, with endurance to match. I knew in advance that the litigation might take years. I had become thirty-two in January 1970, and could not expect my athletic skills to survive prolonged disuse. The proprietors and publicists of baseball could be depended on to remind me of this at every turn, meanwhile reviling me in print as a destroyer, an ingrate, a fanatic, a dupe. As the pressures increased, so would the temptation to surrender. Worse, if I did wave the white flag in exchange for extra money, little effort would be made to publicize that act as a treacherous abandonment of the causes I had resolved to serve. On the contrary, I would be envied as a master negotiator.

According to one doctrine of the young, I was already too old to be trusted. I disagreed. It seemed to me that I saw the world with young eyes. I was offended by the disparity between American reality and American pretension. I wanted reality upgraded, pretension abolished. Above all, I saw life as all of a piece. The hypocrisies of the baseball industry could not possibly have been sustained unless they were symptoms of wider affliction. Wherever I turned, I found fresh evidence that this was so. Baseball was socially relevant, and so was my rebellion against it. The knowledge fueled and fortified me.

During the unquiet spring of 1970, only one man acknowledged in public that my attack on baseball bore implications beyond the game itself. August A. Busch, Jr., is a celebrated beer manufacturer who owns the St. Louis Cardinals, numerous head of Clydesdale horses and other livestock. He seemed to agree that life is all of a piece. With considerable emotion, he advised reporters that he could not fathom what was happening in our country. He declared that my recalcitrance was somehow related to the unrest on American campuses. He was absolutely right. And when he said that he could not understand it, he was absolutely right for the second time in a day.

After deciding to go to court, I notified the Major League Baseball Players Association of my plans and was invited to address a meeting of its executive board. During the question period, Tom Haller of the Los Angeles Dodgers said, "This is a period of black militance. Do you feel that you're doing this as part of that movement? Because you're black?"

A fascinating question, well-meant. If I were white, would I be less sensitive to injustice? Was it inevitable that, of all baseball players, a black man would be the first to rebel? Robert Brown Elliott, of South Carolina, was one of twenty blacks elected to the U.S. House of Representatives during the brief period of democracy that followed the Civil War. Arguing in the House for passage of the country's first civil rights law, Elliott said:

"I regret, sir, that the dark hue of my skin may lend color to the imputation that I am controlled by motives personal to myself in my advocacy of this great measure of national justice. Sir, the motive that impels me is restricted to no such narrow boundary, but is as broad as your Constitution. I advocate it, sir, because it is right."

I told the meeting that organized baseball's policies and practices affected all players equally and that my color was therefore beside the point. It occurred to me later that the answer, while valid, had by no means exhausted the subject. Neither can it be exhausted in this book or even in our time. As I have already suggested, it heartens me to realize that my dispute with baseball will affect more than baseball. I like to believe that I would feel that way even if I were white. To diminish the established insanity in one area of life is to undermine it elsewhere as well. In due course, the quality of justice changes. Values alter. Priorities improve. At the very least, the poor get glass for their windows. One need not be black to appreciate that.

After Larry Albert left, I poked through the mail. Usual bills and brochures—Marian's department. The daily letter to her from Carl, my absent brother. Three letters for me. A child begging an autographed picture. An old ball player wishing me luck. And the third, on lined paper torn from a notebook, began with "Dear Nigger."

The animal informed me that if it were not for the great game of baseball I would be chopping cotton or pushing a broom. And that I was a discredit to my race. By definition, any black hurts his people if he is other than abjectly, supinely, hand-lickingly grateful for having been allowed to earn a decent living.

I assembled a martini, *very* dry. I probably had spoiled the animal's breakfast. I might even have ruined his day. No doubt it had started splendidly, with a front page full of grand news about undesirable elements being bombed, shot, incinerated, beaten, arrested, suspended, expelled, drafted and otherwise coped with here and abroad. Then he must have turned to the sporting page, where horror confronted him. Curt Flood had sued baseball on constitutional grounds. If the newspaper was typical, it lied that a victory for Flood would mean the collapse of our national pastime. God profaned! Flag desecrated! Motherhood defiled! Apple pie blasphemed! The animal was furious. Them niggers is never satisfied.

I am pleased that God made my skin black but I wish He had made it thicker.

2

Your Grandfather and I

I was born in Houston, Texas, on January 18, 1938, the last and least of six children in what now would be classified as a disadvantaged family. When I was about two years old, we moved to Oakland, California, where work was supposed to be more plentiful.

We were not poor, but we had nothing. That is, we ate at regular intervals, but not much. We were not ragged. Both parents lived at home. In the conventially squalid West Oakland ghetto where I grew up, most other households seemed worse off.

To achieve these triumphs of stability, my parents held not fewer than four underpaid jobs at a time. By day, my father was a hospital menial. At night, he moonlighted at the same employment. My mother also was a full-time hospital worker. In the evenings she attended to her own cooking and sewing and cleaning and frugal shopping, and tried to make sense of her children's conflicting reports about the accomplishments, accidents, broken promises, arguments and threats of the day. She had no spare time at all, yet managed to earn extra dollars by mending parachutes on a piecework basis. She often seemed dazed, a condition with which I came to sympathize many years later, after I learned that body and mind can endure only so much.

Because Dad was usually at work and needed desperately to get some rest at home, we seldom saw him except on special occasions like holidays, or when Mother's briefings about our behavior required him to add to his burdens by whipping somebody's ass. I saw him cry about that more than once. He undoubtedly would have preferred other forms of close communication with us. He also would have preferred a living wage for fewer than seventy-two hours of drudgery per week.

Since his immediate responsibilities were more urgent than his preferences, he settled for what he could get. And he gave it all he had. We lived in the two-bedroom apartment of a two-family house. Herman, Barbara, Carl and I occupied one room, each of us with an Army-surplus bunk bed. To sleep in the same room as one's nubile older sister was unremarkable. To have one's own private bed was luxury.

Our other sister, Rickie, about twenty years my senior, lived with her husband in the apartment downstairs. Alvin, our oldest brother, had gone forth into the world by the time I began to keep track of my relatives.

My mother had a thing about fresh fruit. She prized it above other foods and made sure that we got it. This made me a rarity among the infant delinquents with whom I roamed the streets at the age of five or six: I stole fruit for fun. The others stole to relieve hunger. We would sneak around the unloading area at a nearby cannery to grab what we could find. Or we would ambush a fruit truck at a stop light, leap aboard the back, break open a crate, stuff our mouths and pockets and drop to the street before the light turned green.

Beyond the staple fruit, our family table was a marvel of the transformation of nothing into something. Grits, beans, greens and eked-out scraps of hog or fowl are now the basis of what is promoted as soul food at $6 a head. We did not call it soul food. We called it midweek supper. Its only excitement was the suspense of waiting to see whether seconds might be available to fill the vacancy between navel and backbone.

soul food

Because we were so much better off than others, it did not occur to us that our lives were austere. The parents surely knew, but were too busy for lamentation and, in any event, were justifiably proud of what their sacrifices had accomplished. I think I must have been in my middle teens before I discovered that some folks buy new Christmas trees every year. At our place, the festive season became official when Herman Flood, Sr., repaired to the cellar to inspect the previous year's tree, which he had lacquered and hung upside down from a rafter, "to preserve the sap." The durability of the sap may have been theoretical, but not the longevity of my father's $2 tree, which often survived three or four Yules before going hopelessly bald.

He spent more on sketchpads than on Christmas trees. All the kids could draw. Carl and I even seemed to have the makings of artists. It rewarded the parents in their comings and goings, their interminable labors, to see three or four of us sprawled on the living room floor, engrossed in a pastime so remote from the meanness of the streets.

art

Because we were without direct parental supervision most of the time, our affairs were governed by a pecking order in which size and seniority ruled. As undisputed occupant of the lowest position on this totem pole, I amassed a huge inventory of grievances at an early age. Everybody else came first. Not only that, but they seemed to get more. Fury availed me nothing. I was less than convinced that anyone loved me. The phase passed, because it was at odds with reality. But it lasted long enough for me to become a self-sufficiently cool cat. I am a young thirty-two, but I was an old, old eight.

At the age of ten I committed my first and final major crime (unless you count the pilferage of fruit). Prowling the streets alone one day, as was my frequent custom, I came upon a truck parked at a factory. Nobody was around. I climbed into the cab and assumed the position of adult invincibility, hands on steering wheel. A glint caught my eye.

"Hey!" I exulted. "The ignition keys are here! Hey!"

I had played driver a thousand times, but this was for real. Without deliberation or doubt and, as best I can recall, without thought of consequences, I turned the key and the motor started, exactly as I knew it should. Had I not been casing automobiles since I could walk? I managed to reach the clutch. The vehicle rolled forward without major complaint from the gears.

I drove that splendid juggernaut for two entire blocks before it wrested itself from my command and wilfully plowed into a parked car. During the moment between impact and the exquisite knowledge that I had not been killed, my elation diminished abruptly. An hour or so afterward, when the police dropped me at the detention home and I discovered that the door to my room was locked from the outside, I banished bravado forever.

The next morning the door was still locked. Peering through its barred glass window in hope of help or breakfast, I saw my brother Carl walk morosely by. He too had been busted (a bicycle theft, I believe), and did not know that I was a fellow prisoner. This was not his first scrape or his last, but it was the first time that my parents had to retrieve two of their boys on one day. It was a miserable experience for them: Carl twelve, I ten and the whole goddamned environment conspiring to defeat their hopes for us. When we got home, my trembling father told me that I had done $300 worth of damage. He then visited $300 worth of hardship on my behind. It was painful and unnecessary: I had already decided to avoid further traffic with the police. Their locked rooms terrified me. I wanted no more, ever. Carl was a cat of a different stripe. Police and locked rooms offended him and parental whipping humiliated him, but those discomforts only intensified the hurt that drove him. His athlete's body, his huge intelligence and his exuberantly articulate charm were not enough for him. He treated his gifts as if they were a curse. He took awful chances and paid awful prices.

Our parents harbored a version of the American dream. In the manner of the industrious European immigrants with whom American blacks are so frequently and unjustly compared, Herman and Laura Flood ransomed themselves to a vision of the future. Their goal was to raise children upright and industrious enough to qualify for the good life. By this they did not mean riches, influence in the affairs of men, public honor or glittering leisure. Concepts of such magnitude were as alien and unreal as the curiosities projected on the neighborhood movie screen. My mother and father trudged beneath a more modest banner. They hoped that each of us would have a decent job. A loving family. A nicer home on a nicer street. No trouble with the law. No problem with the booze. And, of course, readiness for the better day, the distant day of kindness and opportunity, which would come in Heaven if not on Earth.

By white standards, this was a loser's outlook. By larger standards, it attested to the durability of the human spirit. I am proud of it. I probably cannot influence those whites

who complain that they are tired of feeling guilty about
what their grandfathers did to my grandfathers, but I can
at least suggest that they stop making idiotic comparisons
between my people and European immigrants. I think it
wholesome to bear in mind that American statute and un-
legislated custom not only enslaved my people but outlawed
their languages, their religions and their expressions of
group and individual dignity. Including their desire to form
abiding family relationships. They were bred like cattle.
It is inspiring that so many survived with their finer feelings
intact, after a century of emancipation in which color has
been the badge of ineligibility. To hell with your grand-
father, baby. Just get out of the way.

Although parental sacrifice and its underlying values were
influential, we kids spent the day and much of the night on
the street, amid contrary influences. These were inherently
seductive to begin with, and became more beguiling to the
degree that their dangers were emphasized at home. They
offered quick diversion. They were attuned to the dominant
realities of the environment.

As I have said, ours was a conventionally squalid ghetto.
Those who have not lived in one may have driven through
one. Dozens have been explored on television. As the in-
comparable Agnew has remarked, "when you've seen one,
you've seen 'em all." The usual broken glass, abandoned
furniture and stripped hulks of automobiles littering the
gutters. The noisy, smelly bars. The disheveled whores.
The murderous pushers. The almost ceremonial rolling of
drunks in alleys and hallways. The prevalence of loveless
sex, joyless laughter, endless din, thoughtless violence. A
boy was an oddity if he had not been diddled by the age
of nine and laid by eleven. Probabilities were slight that a
man could emerge from boyhood with a decent view of
love and life.

Every child in the grammar and junior high schools was black. In the national tradition, the curriculum spared us the truth about our heritage. We had once been slaves, the teachers reminded, but now we were free. If anything went wrong, we had only ourselves to blame. Everybody rise and sing *Oh Beautiful for Spacious Skies.*

We saw few whites. None was a bearer of joy. The landlord, storekeeper, cop, teacher, meter reader and the various bill collectors were all enforcers. We accepted their presence, much as a Seminole accepts alligators. They were hazards too familiar for urgent comment. We were so accustomed to things as they were that we seldom speculated about how things ought to have been. When a teacher announced from her remote eminence that the United States was the champion of liberty and the benefactor of world mankind, we scarcely reacted. Such prattle was simply part of the usual distant drone.

Politically sophisticated blacks were trying during the late forties and early fifties to organize the ghetto's paralyzed indignation, but their activities did not penetrate to our level. That sort of thing came much later. I recall little discussion and no excitement in 1954, when the Supreme Court supposedly outlawed the segregation of schools. By then I was sixteen. I think that I would have been aware of local reaction, had there been much. Just as the ghetto warps its victims, it also insulates and lulls them.

Toward the end of World War II, when I was six or seven, I made a gratifying discovery. It seemed that I could outrun any kid on the block. A year or two later, I found that I could catch and throw a ball as expertly as boys twice my age. I was precociously coordinated and mightily impressed. The only better athlete in the immediate vicinity was Carl.

When I was nine, I became the catcher for Junior's

Sweet Shop, in a police-sponsored midget league. Carl was the pitcher. The coach was George Powles, a white man who later became famous for having developed a phenomenal number of outstanding athletes, most of them black. Among the major-league baseball players coached and encouraged by George at McClymonds High School or on his various sandlot and semiprofessional teams were Frank Robinson, Vada Pinson, Billy Martin, Joe Morgan, J.W. Porter, Charles Beamon, Jesse Gonder, Joe Gaines, Chris Cannizzaro and I. He also helped the basketball superstar Bill Russell and the great football players Ollie Matson and John Brodie.

If I now see whites as human beings of variable worth rather than as stereotypes, it is because of a process that began with George Powles. To be sure, black experience teaches that the American white is guilty until he proves himself innocent. No present reason exists to modify this axiom. Our country's prospects might improve if the guilty were less abundant. In time, more blacks might be able to recognize and accept good will when it showed itself. A multitude of George Powleses would accelerate the process.

The beauty of George was that you did not have to adulterate your blackness to win his confidence and approval. He neither preached nor patronized. He emitted none of the smog of the do-gooder embarked on a salvage operation. After the games, he would bring the whole gang of ragamuffins to his pleasant home (a palace!) to plunder his wife's refrigerator. He recently expressed astonishment when somebody told him that I remembered those visits as high points of my childhood. He protested that I had just been one of a crowd of kids and that there had been nothing extraordinary about the doings and that no fuss had been made over me because of my special talents. On reflection, he allowed that ice cream, cookies and comfortable furniture might have made an impression on me. But this had not been noticeable at the time. I was a cool cat.

As I must have sensed then and as is so clear to me now, George Powles had no motives more exalted than good baseball and the benefits it offers. To inspire unfortunates with glimpses of a larger life was furthest from his mind. His home was his home, not a stopover on some inspirational sight-seeing tour for the needy. He just had kids in for ice cream and cookies!

His expectations of a child were based on the child's performance. He raised or lowered his expectations in terms of that criterion and no other. He was genuine.

If my life had turned out differently, the importance of my experience with George Powles might have dwindled. I might have come to regard him as an exception too unusual to matter. But I have had close white friends of a number and quality far beyond reasonable expectation. It is probable that I know more authentically good white people than most white people do.

At Herbert Hoover Junior High School, in Oakland, I met Jim Chambers, an art teacher who absolutely refused to subordinate his love of art and life to the strictures of a dreary educational system. He was a fervently unorthodox young man, appalled by pomposity, inhumanity and pretension. Before I met him, I sketched and painted but had not the slightest sense of the larger significance of art. This was Jim's passion. Because he was jubilant about my skills, and I was avid to learn, he taught me art not as technique alone but as one of the great resources of the human spirit. He aroused in me the sensibilities that finally enable a painter to illuminate life instead of merely illustrating it. He accepted my blackness without fuss. More precisely, he appreciated blackness as a central attribute.

Which reminds me of the spine-chilling remark made

to my sister Barbara by a white man with whom she worked. She was the only black in the office, a state of affairs that aroused discomfort in all. After the novelty began to wear off, she was joined at lunch one day by an expansive white man who paid her the highest compliment in his arsenal. "You know what?" he said, "I don't even *notice* that you're black." She came home undecided whether to cry or laugh. What the white had said, all unknowing, was that he did not accept her for what she was. To make her presence and his own confusions tolerable, he had erased her color from his mind. With it, he had erased her identity. He now was free to interpret her in any way he chose, having dismissed her most apparent characteristic from his consideration.

Jim Chambers and I remained in touch. After I joined the Cardinals, he introduced me to his cousin, Marian Jorgensen, and her husband, Johnny. They crowned my good luck on this earth. They became my dearest friends, my second family. My life with them completed my education on the black-white thing. I now know, and have known for years, that the American black's main problem is not the white as such. And that the main problem of the brainwashed animal who calls me "Dear Nigger" is not the black as such. The problem for us all is the organization of human society. The Man would be no bargain if he were black and the ground rules were otherwise unchanged. Can society get no further than one man's foot on another man's neck? On what basis can we assume that peace and justice would be achieved by substituting a foot of another color? Does the ghetto slum become a more suitable habitation after it falls into the hands of a black landlord? Would war be better if the Secretary of Defense were black?

Before Cassius Clay became Muhammad Ali, Heavyweight Champion of the World, I met him one spring in

Miami. He and the black members of the Cardinals were living in the same segregated motel. He was a lovely kid— bright, amusing and interested in serious conversation. Bob Gibson and I befriended him. Gibson, for the benefit of those who may have strayed into these pages without knowledge of baseball, is one of the greatest pitchers of all time. Also, as will be evident later, he is a marvelous human being. When the young boxer invited us to go to a Black Muslim meeting, we accepted. We both were curious about the Muslims and went with a certain anticipation, I suppose. It would have been wonderful to discover that the sect had a prescription for the nation's ailments.

Our wallets and watches were impounded at the door, possibly to thwart photographic or electronic snooping. Everyone in the hall looked trim, proud, clear-eyed and resolute. The speeches—or sermons—were rampantly, savagely racist. The only discernible program seemed to be destruction of the hated White Devil and substitution of black rule. After Bullet Bob and I got home, he summed it up: "Sounds as if black power would be white power backwards. That wouldn't be much improvement."

Anyone who expects me to attack Muhammad Ali or the Black Muslims can forget it. I respect Ali. Furthermore, I would be surprised if he were a racist fanatic. For all I know, the Muslim oratory is a device to encourage the black pride that I found so evident at the meeting. I simply happen to doubt that black pride need be accomplished by racism. I'm delighted that our kids are finally looking at themselves and saying, "I'm black and I'm beautiful and I'm going to wash this crap out of my hair and stop trying to jump into the white man's bag." Great. But we ought to have learned enough about racism to avoid it in ourselves.

The saddest thing about black racism is that The Man

doesn't really mind it much. Of what possible danger to the existing order are lunatics who scream that 10 percent of the population should overpower the other 90?

If ever there has been a busier little boy than I was during my school days, he probably ended in a rest home. I did all the scenery for the school plays. I painted house numbers on porches, stoops and curbs for five cents per digit. I decorated show windows for a warmly generous baseball enthusiast, Sam Bercovich. I pursued girls and caught my share. I read an occasional schoolbook and scraped by without distinction but without serious mishaps. When Barbara separated from her husband, I moved into her place so that she could take a night job without having to hire baby-sitters.

Baseball was my deal. I had become unquenchably fired up at nine when I not only played for Junior's Sweet Shop but served as mascot of a championship American Legion team coached by George Powles. He let me give exhibitions of fancy fielding before the Legion games. I raced all over the diamond like a terrier, gobbling up every ball I could reach. The applause warmed me. If I had ever been short of self-esteem, the problem disappeared in the recognition I got for doing something socially acceptable and doing it well.

When school was out, I played ball from dawn to sunset at Poplar Playground, a ghetto park, unless I was scheduled elsewhere with one of George's teams. It went on like that for years. This emphasis on sport, plus all the other things I had to do, set me apart from most of the neighborhood kids. It probably was just as well. I went my own way. Some may have felt, some may even have hoped that I was headed for the crushing defeat that, in ghetto experience, awaited all strivers, all blacks who tried to better

themselves. I did not think of it that way at all. I was not
striving. I was just doing what I liked.

In my mid-teens, I began to suspect that I might be able
to make a living in baseball. At McClymonds High School
and then at Oakland Technical (to which I had been
required to transfer when I moved to Barbara's), I was
something of a star. With Frank Robinson and Vada Pinson, I helped George Powles win American Legion championships for the Bill Irwin Post. I also played for George
on his Bercovich team in the Alameda Winter League,
competing against seasoned professionals, including some
with major-league credentials. I did not hit the ball as hard
as Frank Robinson, who had always been the biggest and
most powerful of us, and I was not as fleet as Vada, but I
had not yet seen a team for which I could not play. With
experience, I might even be able to make the Oakland Oaks
of the Pacific Coast League. The big leagues were too
unreal to dwell upon.

Professional scouts began coming around to chat. None
seemed overwhelmed by my prospects, but all were interested enough to inspect me at close range and appraise my
personality. I have been told that I was in those days a
fetching mix of cool confidence and adolescent eagerness.
Seems plausible. I recall having felt that way most of the
time, and I am sure that I was artful enough to project
the best possible vibrations to those sharp-eyed white men
with influence back East.

One day George Powles sat me down for a talk. He told
me that I had the ability to become a professional, but that
I should prepare for difficulties and disappointments. He
pointed out that I weighed barely 140 pounds, was not
more than five feet, seven inches tall and, in the language
of the time, a Negro. Small men seldom got very far in
baseball. And black men not only had to play better than

whites of equal experience but were unlikely to get much
of a chance unless they looked almost certain to make good.
Accordingly, a small, black youth was well advised to steel
himself. If I got a chance and made the most of it, I might
indeed be able to earn my way in the game. But nothing
would be made easy for me. Ever. Some people would look
down on me, no matter what I accomplished.

He was telling me the facts of life. It was characteristic
of his friendship. He was neither maudlin nor indignant. I
understood exactly what he was saying and believed it. But
he was describing a terrain beyond my emotional ken, like
a man telling another about Copenhagen. To feel Copenhagen one must either see it for oneself or relate it to something similar already seen. I had spent my boyhood in the
shelter of the ghetto and in the isolation of the baseball
park. I truly did not *know*, I did not know in my bones
that I had been discriminated against from birth. Fully to
know and feel the penalties of blackness, I would have to
experience something new, the onslaught of the outside
world. But I did not even know that.

With the approach of my eighteenth birthday and grad-
uation from high school, I had to choose between baseball
and an attempt to scrounge a job in commercial art. It was
an easy choice. Art could wait. And college did not even
enter the deliberations. The time had come for me to con-
tribute substantial money to the family.

Bobby Mattick, of the Cincinnati Reds, was the only
scout interested enough in my services to negotiate for
them. He did not consider me too small. Perhaps he
thought that I would grow. He visited our house several
times and finally offered me a salary of $4,000 to spend the
season of 1956 in the Cincinnati organization. He promised
me a real chance with a superior minor-league team, just
as Frank Robinson had been given during 1955. Moreover,

I would begin the spring training season as a member of the Reds themselves. I would train with the big shots at the Cincinnati camp in Tampa. No bonus was offered me for signing, and none was asked. I was lucky to get an opportunity at all.

In February 1956, a new diploma tucked safely away at home, I walked aboard an airplane and set forth for Tampa. I was keyed up, but I had not felt fright in years. I knew that I could play baseball. I looked forward to joining Frank Robinson again. It would be like old times.

3

Adventures in the Bush

According to the brochure mailed to me by the Cincinnati Reds, the players lived at the Floridian Hotel during the spring training season. Sounded fancy. I would check in, grab a shower, find Frank Robinson and inspect the town. Man, we had come a long way from Poplar Playground. Maybe Frank and I would room together and play side by side in the outfield. Maybe we both would make the big team.

The airplane landed in one piece. I had survived my first flight. I was becoming sophisticated. As I floated toward the baggage-claim area, I saw the drinking fountains. One was labeled "White," and the other, "Colored." For a wild instant I wondered whether the signs meant club soda and Coke. The truth struck, like a door slammed in my face. I had heard of such drinking fountains and here they were. Thank goodness I was just passing through on my way to the Floridian and baseball.

The hotel lobby impressed me. I was going to like it

here. Real major-league accommodations. I presented myself to the desk clerk. "I believe you have reservations for Mr. Flood," I said urbanely.

Whitely, he looked at my face. Bleakly, he looked at my new suit.

"You with the ball team?"

"Yes."

He averted his eyes and yelled to somebody backstage. "Hey! This boy here with the ball team. You know where to send him." He then disappeared.

Presently a black porter emerged from behind the desk and beckoned me. I followed him through the lobby to a side door and found myself on the street. He waved me into a cab and told the black driver, "Ma Felder's."

Until it happens you literally cannot believe it. After it happens, you need time to absorb it. The black cab took me five miles out of town and deposited me at Mrs. Felder's boardinghouse. When I saw who was there—Frank Robinson and four or five other black ball players—my knees began to knock. Rules had been invoked and enforced. I was at Ma Felder's because white law, white custom and white sensibility required me to remain offstage until wanted. I was a good athlete and might have an opportunity to show it, but this incidental skill did not redeem me socially. Officially and for the duration, I was a nigger.

Ma Felder's other guests were stoking up with fatty ham, collard greens and black-eyed peas. They welcomed me with thoughtful grins and soft handshakes. All were older than I. Some, like Joe Black, Brooks Lawrence, Pat Scantlebury and Charlie Harmon, were much older. I choked back my revelations about the drinking fountains and the white hotel. These men had been that route and bore the scars in their eyes. They reminded me of aging gladiators weeping over one another's wounds. I now was one of them, preparing to fight them for my own survival yet bound to them in the outraged tenderness of brotherhood. As the youngest, newest and, for all I knew, the most vulnerable, I could not afford the trembling numbness which had seized me when I entered that house. I needed to get myself together in a hurry or my professional baseball career would end before it started.

The management of the Cincinnati Reds seemed to appreciate my work on the playing field. I won mention in a few newspaper stories. It seemed to me that I was clearly the best fielder on the squad and that major-league pitching would present no great problems after I had seen enough of it. By the time I was shipped to the club's minor-league training center at Douglas, Georgia, I was satisfied that I would play center field for the Reds after a year or two of seasoning.

The Georgia camp was a former Army air base and retained the G.I. flavor. More than four hundred candidates for jobs in the Cincinnati farm system lived in its barracks, which included a segregated one for the likes of me. They blew us awake with reveille at 7 A.M. and kept us at a regimented gallop for most of the day. Each player wore a numbered placard on his back, enabling the management's walking bosses to record every significant move without stopping to ask names. My number was 330, hinting that other players had come more immediately to mind when placards were issued. This aborted complacence. With a lower number I might easily have taken success for granted. The quality of the baseball at Douglas was distinctly inferior to that of the Alameda Winter League.

The nights were rich in cultural opportunity. If we untouchables cared for the movies, we were welcome to sit by ourselves in the balcony. The town also offered a couple of black bars, which sold bootleg moonshine and were frequented by sluts. You hardly dared breathe in those dives, for fear of venereal infection of the respiratory tract. Still, the places were sanctuaries. Our white overseers did not enter the black neighborhood, much less patrol its bars.

Eighteen-year-old players and others of unestablished talent usually started their careers in the Class D leagues, the lowest of the low minors. The Reds assigned me to the High Point–Thomasville club in the Carolina League, which was Class B. Apparently I had made a good impression. I was beginning to feel like myself again. It would be good in North Carolina. I would find a nice apartment. I would establish myself in the community. I would proceed to the fame and riches that awaited me. After only one year of minor-league experience, Frank Robinson had just been promoted to the Reds. I could hope to do as well.

As I rode the bus to my new home, I saw myself returning there in later years, burdened with prominence. Dear friends, including many girls, would wave at me from the curbs. Substantial citizens would slap each other on the back, proud that good old Curt had come to pay them a visit. I would have lunch with the mayor, dedicate the new library, endow an animal hospital and give all the little children rides in my new Rolls-Royce.

I was ready for High Point–Thomasville, but the two peckerwood communities were not ready for me. Or maybe they were. One of my first and most enduring memories is of a large, loud cracker who installed himself and his four little boys in a front-row box and started yelling "black bastard" at me. I noticed that he eyed the boys narrowly, as if to make sure that they were learning the correct intonation. Wherever we played in that league, at home or away, the stadiums resounded with "nigger," "eight-ball," "jigaboo" and other pleasantries.

At Fayetteville, North Carolina, I heard spluttering

gasps: "There's a goddamned nigger son-of-a-bitch playing
ball with them white boys! I'm leaving."

The few blacks in these audiences included a demoralized
handful who seemed to enjoy echoing their oppressors.
Some cracker would bawl at me, "Move yo' ass, snowball!"
and, sure enough, a boozy voice—separate but briefly equal
—would pipe from the Jim Crow section, "Move yo' ass,
snowball!"

Most of the players on my team were offended by my
presence and would not even talk to me when we were off
the field. The few who were more enlightened were afraid
to antagonize the others. The manager, whose name merci-
fully escapes me, made clear that his life already was sufficiently difficult without contributions from me. I was
entirely on my own.

We played eight games a week: every night from Monday though Saturday, plus a double-header on Sunday
afternoon. Wherever we were, I lived and ate in the local
equivalent of Ma Felder's. When we were in transit and
the team bus made a dinner stop, I was not permitted in
the dining room. I had to go to the back door of the restaurant, like a beggar. I also was barred from the rest rooms.
If I needed to relieve myself, the bus would stop along the
highway and I would hide from traffic as best I could while
wetting a rear wheel.

What had started as a chance to test my baseball ability
in a professional setting had become an obligation to
measure myself as a man. As such, it was a matter of life
and death. These brutes were trying to destroy me. If they
could make me collapse and quit, it would verify their
preconceptions. And it would wreck my life.

During the early weeks of the season, I used to break
into tears as soon as I reached the safety of my room. I felt
too young for the ordeal. I wanted to be home. I wanted to

talk to someone. I wanted to be free of these animals whose fifty-cent bleacher ticket was a license to curse my color and deny my humanity. I wanted to be free of the imbeciles on the ball team.

Regardless of the emphasis that its publicists place on individual heroics, baseball is a team game. One moment of distraction, one muffed catch or one poor throw can scramble the entire pattern and lose the game. Given reasonable skill to begin with, the player's most critical attribute is his ability to concentrate. If he feels as one with his teammates, he is caught up in a spirit of joyous cooperation. His reflexes sharpen. His body excels itself. Without this spirit, his adrenals doze. He cannot make the big plays.

For me, conventional team spirit was out of the question. My teammates despised and rejected me as subhuman. I gladly would have sent them all to hell. More than once during that horrible season, I was tempted to strike out so that our cracker pitcher would lose another game. More than once, I almost threw the ball away or dropped a fly for the same vengeful purpose.

If I did not sabotage the team (and I never did), it was only because I had been playing baseball too long and too well to discredit myself. And I was too black. Pride was my resource. I solved my problem by playing my guts out. I ran myself down to less than 135 pounds in the blistering heat. I completely wiped out that peckerwood league. I led it in everything but home runs—although I hit 29. I played in all 154 games. I batted .340, driving in 128 runs with 190 hits. The better I did, the tougher I got. I no longer wept in my room.

Toward midseason, when I had established myself as a star, I attended to another matter of importance. During the pregame practice one evening, a little black kid jumped onto the field, grabbed a loose ball, and climbed back into the stands. One of our lint-head pitchers screamed, "Hey you black nigger, come back with that ball!" Then he jumped into the stands, took the ball from the child and returned to the field, flushed with triumph. I was waiting for him.

"Don't use that word around me," I said. "You owe me more respect than that. White kids steal baseballs all the time without interference, you wool-hat son-of-a-bitch. If you ever come near me again you'll be sorry."

I would have killed him without regret. I was hoping that he would swing at me, but he skulked off and gave me a wide berth for the rest of the season. His peers became more civil now that they sensed my rage. By the end of the year I had even begun to adjust to the abuse from the stands. I had developed explanations for the behavior of the fans. They were little men. The opportunity to insult a baseball player made them grow a few inches. They were not worth my contempt. Who cared about them? And so forth. None of these rationalizations could have stood close scrutiny, but they worked. I became cooler and cooler. When you have answered insult and rejection with a .340 batting average, you have done something more than philosophical. Especially when you are sure that your achievements have emancipated you from North Carolina for keeps. I believe that I would have quit baseball rather than return there.

At the end of the 1956 season, I joined the Reds for a few days, some of which were spent playing in New York. Lo and behold, the entire team roomed at the Biltmore, as if blacks were members of the human race. I wrote breezy letters on hotel stationery to my family and friends in Oakland. Jim Chambers kept one and showed it to me not long ago. It bragged callowly of the pleasures and privileges of being big-league. It implied that I was happily occupied with an abundance of eager girls. How quickly the spirit heals at eighteen! Girls had been available in the Carolina League, but I had been less than joyful about them. I had expended rage in forbidden beds. I did not want to marry the peckerwood's sister. The question never arose. She was always scratching at my door.

One afternoon during the final days of the Cincinnati season, I was called to the office of Gabe Paul, general manager of the Reds. As my first employers, the Reds now had exclusive rights to my baseball services for as long as they chose to retain them. I could play only where they elected to send me. This was baseball law. It was beyond question or dispute. It was taken entirely for granted. And it was a powerful factor in salary negotiations between the player and his club. It still is.

I reminded Paul of my accomplishments in the Carolina League. As I mentioned each statistic, his head shook slowly from side to side in melancholy negation. I pressed on, not knowing what else to do, and ended by announcing that I was entitled to a raise in pay.

I thought the man's heart would break when he replied that a raise was out of the question. He agreed that I had done a pretty fair job, for a beginner. But confidentially, the club's expenses were dangerously out of hand. Son, the Reds were in deep trouble. They simply did not have the money, son. To keep the team alive, we all had to tighten our belts and be patient. At the same time we had to develop ourselves as rapidly as possible, so that we could bring a National League pennant to Cincinnati and make money for us all. Those who put their shoulders to the wheel would be rewarded. Son, make no mistake about it. He was confident that he could count on my good sense. He was confident that I would realize that I was not yet ready for the major leagues, and that my most significant contribution to the well-being of the club would come by working hard, seeing the big picture, taking the long view and not becoming impatient. The constructive thing to do was sign a 1957 contract for $4,000, accept promotion to a higher minor league and do my very, very best. I wanted to be well thought of. I agreed.

I wanted to get away from baseball for the first time in my life. My adventures in North Carolina had depleted me. I looked forward to a long winter in Oakland. But the Reds had other ideas. To accelerate my progress, they ordered me to play a season of winter baseball in the Dominican Republic. Neither spirit nor flesh was willing. I tried to generate some enthusiasm, but I came up empty. I played so badly that the Dominican team released me after a couple of weeks. I was too strung out to care about the stain on my record. I retreated to Oakland and slept for days. When I arrived at Ma Felder's in February 1957, I had recovered fully. I felt like a tiger.

This time the Reds farmed me out to Savannah in the Class A South Atlantic League. The Georgia city had lately been in a high state of tension about school desegregation and other civil rights. When I saw how uptight the black community was, and how hostile the whites were, I realized that Cincinnati had arranged another full dose for me.

The only available accommodations were in a dormitory at Savannah State College, a segregated school. I worked at night, when the students were off, and slept during the day, when they went to class. The one other black man on our team was Leo Cardenas, a Cuban for whom lodgings had been found with a Spanish-speaking family. I anticipated a second lonely summer and got it.

Cardenas could speak almost no English. His bafflement about the customs of the region was inexpressible. Time and again, when we were walking down the street of a

Southern town, Leo would point to a comfortable-looking restaurant and say, "We go there."

"We can't," I'd reply.

"Why?"

"They don't like us."

"*Like?*"

"They don't want us."

"Why they no want us?"

"They don't want black people."

"Why?"

After our night games at the Savannah ball park, Leo would flee to his Spanish sanctuary. He remained fairly happy all summer, drawing comfort from the leisure hours he spent with countrymen. Furthermore, they fed him. I was jealous. The one eating place open to me at night was the Jim Crow lunchroom in the bus terminal. It may have been the smelliest, greasiest, grimiest restaurant in the world. I went there assuming that indigestion was preferable to starvation. Confronted by the unspeakable food, I often changed my mind. One night the large manager-cook-waitress-cashier-dishwasher looked at my untouched plate. "Something wrong?" I could not bring myself to answer.

Georgia law forbade Cardenas and me to dress with the white players. A separate cubicle was constructed for us. Some of the players were decent enough to detest the arrangement. I particularly remember Buddy Gilbert, who used to bring food to me and Leo in the bus, so that we would not have to stand at the back doors of restaurants. I felt sorry for him—he obviously was ashamed of his helplessness. "Curt," he'd say, "I wish it wasn't like this." Sometimes I would try to give it the light touch, but we both knew I did not have my heart in it. Of the many indignities to which I was subject, few angered me more completely than the routine in that bus. After playing a

double-header in some piney woods clearing, it was absolutely maddening to sit all sweaty and sticky and funky in
that rotten bus instead of walking like a human being into
a restaurant. Poor Gilbert's small kindnesses only accentu-
ated the cruelty of prejudice.

The crowds in the larger cities of the South Atlantic
League were not always as blatant as those in the North
Carolina mill towns. The cries of "nigger" and "snowball"
were constant, but not so frequent or loud as in the back-
woods league. I was not yet accustomed to this kind of
treatment, and never would be, yet I had toughened with
experience. The emotional impact was not as severe as it
had been during the previous season. I was going to be a
professional entertainer on the big wheel, by God, and these
crackers would not stop me.

The Reds thought that they needed a new third baseman, and ordered the Savannah management to use me at
that position. Anything that promised to hasten my ad-
vancement was agreeable to me, even though I knew that
my real talents were in the outfield. I got 170 hits that year,
ended with a batting average of .299 and was named to the
league's All-Star team. Once again I was called to Cincinnati for the final days of the season. This time, I got my first
major-league hit, a home run off Moe Drabowsky of the
Chicago Cubs.

When I entered Gabe Paul's office for the ritual of negotiation, I was almost buoyant. He was not. In fact, he
was sadly disappointed that my batting average had declined by forty-one points. He and others had been so
hopeful that I would show improvement. But they were
willing to give me another chance. No, he would go further
than that: They were *eager* to give me another chance.
Some people might lose faith in me, but not my staunch
friends and well-wishers in the Cincinnati organization.

Did I think that I might prove deserving of their faith by showing improvement during 1958? Yes, yes, yes, Mr. Paul. The thought of demanding a salary increase had been banished from my mind.

Paul informed me that Don Hoak had come up with a big year at third base, and that the Reds no longer felt any urgency about preparing me for that job. On the other hand, the team's great second baseman, Johnny Temple, was getting on in years. It was vital that I acquaint myself with his line of work. Paul therefore had arranged for me to spend the winter at second base under Johnny Temple's management in Maracaibo, Venezuela. I went quietly.

It took me a month to recover from dysentery, which knocked me endwise almost as soon as I arrived in South America. Temple tried patiently to make a second baseman of me, but I was not much good at it. My second summer in the gallant South had drained me, and the trots supplied the finishing touches. I tried to cooperate with Johnny, who treated me nicely, but we both recognized that the experiment was not going well.

I began to appreciate Leo Cardenas for what he had gone through in a strange land. To be sure, nobody was discriminating against me on account of my color. This permitted me to spare some attention for the heat, which I hated, and the drinking water, in which I could see organisms multiplying. I could not converse with the broads, which grieved me. I was afraid of the food. Venezuela was one mad continuous round of pleasure. I had no hostility toward the country, but would have been content to return immediately to Oakland and let the Venezuelans shift for themselves.

The proprietors of Venezuelan baseball teams were terribly concerned about the game's image. A player suspected of sexual intercourse could count on hardship from the front office. Detectives followed us around all the time, policing our fun. The players managed, as players will, sneaking off to whorehouses at nine in the morning, before the gumshoes reported for duty. My roommate, a sadly disorganized black from the States, returned from one of these excursions with a dose of the clap.

After he described the symptoms, which mystified him, I advised him to see a doctor. He did. A week later, he reported a recurrence of symptoms. Under questioning, he admitted that he had been back to the house. Not only that, he had balled the same girl.

"You nut!" I cried. "You knew she had the clap!"

"It was worth it," he said dreamily.

One morning about four, I heard him get out of bed and leave the room. As his self-appointed warden, I followed. He went to the hotel swimming pool and began running briskly around it, backwards.

"What now?" I inquired.

"Good practice, Curt," he said without missing a step. "In case they ever ask me to play first base, I'll be ready to run backwards like a first baseman."

He later proved to be a psychotic, the first I met in baseball, but not the last.

The brave attempt to make me a second baseman ended hilariously. As Johnny Temple and I were preparing to leave for the ball park one day, an envelope was slipped under his door. After finding that the only English in it was his name, Johnny stuffed the message in his back pocket. In the locker room he asked one of the Latin-Americans to translate.

The player read the letter with obvious relish.

"What's it say?" asked John.

"You fire," grinned the player.

"What?"

"You fire," roared the player, holding his sides. "It from

the big boss. Owner of club. He say you fire. You all through."

Let us hear no more talk about backward nations. When it comes to cuffing the help, the Latin baseball entrepreneur yields nothing in grace and aplomb to his gringo counterpart.

Then came a wire from Gabe Paul. I had been traded to the St. Louis Cardinals. The Reds wished me luck. Hail and farewell. I learned later that Cincinnati had been impressed by Vada Pinson's work during his first minor-league season, 1957. Because he was the bigger of us, and the faster, and because they neither needed me for third base nor cared particularly for an all-black outfield of Robinson, Pinson and Flood, they unloaded me to the Cards.

During the hullabaloo that followed the announcement of my lawsuit against baseball, a few reporters pointed out triumphantly that I had neglected to sue the Reds when they traded me in 1957. Implication: Flood's 1970 attitudes were freshly minted, opportunistic and inconsistent. Answer: I did not sue the Reds in 1957 because the possibility did not even occur to me. If it had, I would not have dared to act on it.

I was a nobody. Not only that, I was a nobody unwanted by the Reds. Gabe Paul had told me what a grand family they were. I had aspired to a place at the table but had been shown the door instead. Where had I failed Big Daddy? If there was anger in me when I got the telegram, sorrow swamped it. I wondered if the Cardinals would like me. I wondered if I could fit in. I wondered if they would send me to another minor league in the South, and if I could stand another year in that hell.

But to my amazement, the new dealer broke out a fresh deck and dealt me a beautiful hand. The Cardinals sent me a $5,000 contract. A 25 percent raise!

4

Geniuses Need Not Apply

According to the mythology in which they swaddle the
minds of their customers and employees, the owners
of major-league baseball are philanthropists. These dedicated men are custodians of a great tradition, the slightest
neglect of which would plunge the entire United States
into degradation.

Their gravest concern is the Good of the Game. With
this in mind, they maintain constant vigil over the Integrity
of the Game—its competitive honesty and fairness. And
they cultivate the Image of the Game, having realized long
ago that what the public perceives, or thinks it perceives,
need not always correspond to reality. If reality becomes
an inconvenience, it can be camouflaged.

Everyone in baseball plays a structured role in the promotional rites that emphasize the Integrity, enhance the Image
and consolidate the Good of the Game. On camera or
within earshot of working reporters, the behaved player is

an actor who projects blissful contentment, inexhaustible
optimism and abiding gratitude.

"I'll sweep out the clubhouse to stay here," he says. "I
love the game. I owe everything to baseball. I am thankful
to this grand organization for giving me my big chance. I'm
in love with this town and its wonderful fans. Even though
I had kind of a slow start, I think I'm getting it all together,
now. I expect to have a big year."

A player courts trouble if his public pronouncements
stray too far from that familiar vein. Jim Brosnan, a competent pitcher, was unable to find big-league employment
after he wrote mildly irreverent books and articles about
baseball. More recently, Jim Bouton published a quite
revealing book and was called onto the carpet of Bowie K.
Kuhn, whose job as Commissioner of Baseball makes him
chief curator of the Integrity, Image and Good of the
Game. It was made clear to Bouton that when truth challenges mythology a wise ball player keeps his mouth shut.
Bouton had to know this to begin with. Most players do.
It is spelled out in their contracts:

"In addition to his services in connection with the actual
playing of baseball, the Player agrees to cooperate with the
Club and participate in any and all promotional activities
of the Club and its League, which, in the opinion of the
Club, will promote the welfare of the Club or professional
baseball, and to observe and comply with all requirements
of the Club respecting conduct and service of its team and
its players, at all times whether on or off the field."

The only approved posture is one of tail-wagging thanks
for the opportunities provided by the employer. Few active
players feel anything like such gratitude, and none has
reason to. Baseball employment is too insecure for that.
Not many players deliver their ceremonial recitations without a sense of embarrassment.

Like other showfolk, the player usually understands the commercial necessity of kidding the public. He is willing enough to cooperate in that regard if only to be in on the joke. What burns him is the awareness that certain of his contributions to the fables of baseball strengthen the employer's position and weaken his own. For example, baseball has managed to persuade its public that *good* players are superhumanly selfless. On and off the field, their first thought is the well-being of the team (as the contract emphasizes). Accordingly, a player becomes suspect when he postpones his arrival at the spring training camp while attempting to negotiate an equitable contract for himself. The delay in his conditioning supposedly endangers the Club. This betrays him as more concerned with his own good than with the Good of the Game. No *good* player behaves like that. Players who do can count on getting the works from the press.

The typical player would not be in the big leagues at all if he were not highly competitive. He could hardly qualify for his job if he had not been obsessed with baseball since early childhood. In cultivating his talents to a professional level, he probably neglected crucial aspects of his intellectual and emotional development. He may regret this in time. His major-league career lasts, on the average, less than five years. This is his reward for a lifetime of single-minded concentration on baseball technique. To remain on the scene for even that meager span requires utmost effort. One does not compete against the best without constantly trying to surpass oneself. The pace is frantic. The hours are unnatural. The strain is enormous.

The player almost certainly suffers from stress-connected disturbances of the digestive tract. The chances are large that he also has spells of insomnia. He probably uses tranquilizers and pep pills. If he is married, it is a safe bet that his wife is discontented, jangled and advisedly suspicious. Their tensions are heightened by his absolute lack of job security. He never knows when he might be required to uproot his family to move to a new city, without the slightest assurance of tenure there.

If he allows any of these concerns to affect his play, his career will end the sooner. But not before the press has bewailed his deterioration and—if the team management chooses—has even cast doubt on his dedication to the Game, thus lessening his ability to get a fair price for his services elsewhere. On the other hand, if he continues to play adequately and is lucky enough to help his team win a few games, he may well be lauded as that paragon of nineteenth-century Integrity—the Hungry Ball Player. The Hungry Ball Player is Good for the Game. As long as he continues to play his desperate best, drives in some important runs and, above all, remains hungry, he has a good chance to prolong his welcome in the major leagues. Lacking star quality, however, he runs serious risks when he tries to meet his needs by demanding a substantial increase in pay. Only a narrow margin separates the Hungry Ball Player from the Ingrate.

Under the ideological guidance of baseball's proprietors, an astonishingly high proportion of our sports reporters become incensed when a young man with a career expectancy of five years undermines the Good of the Game by holding out for a $25,000 salary. Admittedly, sports reporters do not usually get $25,000 a year from their own employers and, furthermore, are sometimes capable of larger contributions to society than might be expected from a journeyman ball player. If this kind of comparison is on their minds, as it seems to be, I wish they would carry it further.

For example, a young reporter's career expectancy might well be forty years. If he decides to leave newspapering, or

is discharged, his education and experience qualify him to
enter a related field at no loss of pay. But the ball player
who does not want to continue disemboweling himself
for $15,000 a year may have few alternatives. And the
washed-up player often confronts a dead end. The last I
heard of Sam Jones, an excellent pitcher for twelve years,
he was considering a job in the West Virginia coal mines.
It was not an executive position.

All but a very few major leaguers share my view of baseball reality. Among those who do not, the most prominent
is the great Willie Mays, who reports from the privileged
isolation of his huge success that he has absolutely nothing
to complain about. The most vociferous champion of the
status quo is Carl Yastrzemski, a go-getter for whom a
bright future is predicted in the upper reaches of baseball
administration. Among former stars who differ with me,
Stan Musial should be included. We played side by side
for eight years, occupied space in the same locker room,
negotiated with the same employer and, within those limits,
had experiences in common. But he had other things going
for him.

Stan was one of the outstanding players of all time. He
was so exceptionally talented, popular and durable that
he played for twenty-one seasons, amassed substantial
wealth and became a member of the Cardinal management.
As an authentic superstar, he lived remote from the difficulties encountered by lesser athletes. Like Mays, he saw
the world entirely in terms of his own good fortune. He was
convinced that it was the best of all possible worlds. He
not only accepted baseball mythology but propounded it.
Whereas the typical player all but choked while reciting
the traditional gibberish of gratitude to the industry, and
whereas Bob Gibson, superstar of another hue, would
simply change the subject, Musial was a true believer.

Gibson and I once clocked eight "wunnerfuls" in a Musial speech that could not have been longer than a hundred words.

"My biggest thrill is just wearing this major-league uniform," Stan used to say. "It's wunnerful being here with all these wunnerful fellas."

On such occasions, Gibson would hang his head in embarrassment and mutter, "Shitfuckpiss." We admired Musial as an athlete. We liked him as a man. There was no conscious harm in him. He was just unfathomably naive. After twenty years of baseball, his critical faculties were those of a schoolboy. After twenty years, he was still wagging his tail for the front office—not because he felt it politic to do so, but because he believed every word he spoke.

A key figure in baseball's promotional pageant is, of course, the manager. Whether interviewed in print, on radio or television, he comes across as wise and guileful and, in some cases, attractively grizzled. Whatever the quality *management* of his team, the fans sense that the old warrior really knows the game and is a sage handler of men. Or—as management was inclined to call all players before the black influx amended the language—"boys." He may be gruff, but a player can turn to him for good counsel. Not just to improve the batting average or sharpen the curve ball, mind you, but for more personal concerns, like making wise investments or naming the baby. Three days after the interview, when the front office fires that manager to atone for its own failure to assemble a winning team, the fan is reminded that managerial turnover is standard practice. Part of the game. Thoroughly acceptable. Happens all the time. Besides, the dismissed manager was too gruff. Or not gruff enough.

After decades of such bullshit, the loyal fan knows ex-

actly as much and no more about the inner workings of
baseball as the industry deems advisable. Which is not very
much, and often is beside the point. To understand baseball at all, and make reasonable demands of it, the fan
must bear in mind that baseball is show business. Their
protestations notwithstanding, the owners measure the
Good of the Game in terms of the profits that remain after
expenses are subtracted from receipts. Everything else is
subordinated, including the quality of what takes place on
the playing field.

The proprietors of baseball have never hesitated to adulterate the game to make an extra dollar. Exhibit A is the
profitably extended season of 162 games, plus preseason
exhibitions, plus in-season exhibitions, plus intraleague
championship playoffs, plus a World Series that has become a travesty because the men are utterly exhausted
before it starts.

The new stadiums of which baseball is so proud con-
stitute Exhibit B. None enhances the quality of play. For
one thing, they are triumphs of thrifty design, built like
football bowls, not baseball parks. Lacking the roof over-
hangs that shade the white shirts of the audience in a conventional stadium, the new bowls present the fielders with
serious problems. Extra split seconds are required to locate
a fly ball against the bright background. Any owner genuinely concerned with playing conditions would not field
a team in a setting with such defects.

At San Francisco's Candlestick Park, the construction of
which involved a land-fill deal that scandalized the community, high winds raise havoc. Pop flies careen in the
gusts, drop maddeningly to the ground and become extra-
base hits. It is hard to determine how this particular stadium can be justified by an industry whose spokesmen are
forever invoking the Integrity of the Game.

The Houston Astrodome is scarcely better, although it has a roof. It is entirely windless and might be expected to rank at the other extreme. Nevertheless, it is worth your life to try to catch a pop fly there. When we first played in the Astrodome the glare from the translucent dome was blinding. Routine fly balls plummeted uncaught like shot ducks. To remedy this, some genius ordered that the roof be tinted. The chosen color was most attractive—the exact color of a baseball. A pop fly remained invisible through much of its flight—white on white.

Exhibit C would be the synthetic playing surfaces now being installed in major-league stadiums. Their only merits are economic. They cost less to maintain than sod. And they permit play (of a sort) in wet weather, thereby reducing costly cancellations. The new surfaces are almost as resilient as rubber. Gently batted balls skip all the way to the outfield fences, like flat stones across a pond. In summer sun, the plastic becomes hot enough to blister skin. Wherever such a field exists, quality suffers. The owners accept this state of affairs calmly because it affects their profits favorably.

Exhibit D would be the curious lack of true competition among the rugged individualists who own the teams. In contrast with the headlong ferocity demanded of players, the owners display toward one another a solicitude that can only be described as tender. Like members of a cartel, or Mafia, they accord each other little conveniences. During the era when the invincibility of the New York Yankees meant box-office profits for their rivals as well, both major leagues seemed to outdo themselves to keep the Yankees invincible. Every year, the New York club managed to obtain the one topnotch player it needed for another pennant. Miracles of barter brought Johnny Mize, Johnny Hopp, Johnny Sain, Bob Turley and Bobby Shantz, to name the few I can recall. Also, in brave immunity from what the naive might have considered to be the Integrity of the Game, the Yankees were permitted for years to use the Kansas City Athletics, a supposed enemy in the American League, as a private farm club. Whoever looked adequate on the Kansas City team wound up in a Yankee uniform. Like Roger Maris.

In 1967, after the Cardinals won the National League pennant by ten games, laughing all the way, the league's heavy thinkers must have decided that a repeat performance would endanger the Good of the Game. What happened next can be taken as evidence that even the most rugged individualist is capable of suppressing his own appetite when the common good is at stake. The National League playing schedule for 1968 looked as if it had been designed for the single purpose of beating the Cardinals out of another pennant.

Our team was required to play fifty-seven consecutive games, without a single day of rest, during the hottest weeks of July and August. What galled us was that the Cardinal management concurred in the adoption of that schedule. It did not even murmur sympathetically when we players squawked. Inasmuch as we won the 1968 pennant despite the schedule, some might think that our beefs were unfounded and that the whole episode merely proved management's superior wisdom. It was hinted that I and others should have bitten our tongues for suspecting the management of conspiring against its own team. Still, if it was not collusion it might just as well have been. The anger that drove us through that killing schedule was not enough to win the World Series. By Series time we had nothing left. We lost in seven games to a Detroit team that we might have defeated in five if we had been physically fit.

For another striking example of the readiness with which the owners subordinate competitive fervor to the greater good of profitable cooperation, I offer the peculiar West Coast schedules with which the National League used to make Walter O'Malley's Los Angeles Dodgers look better than they were. An Eastern team that invaded the Far West did not fly to San Francisco and then to Los Angeles and then to Houston and then homeward. Neither did it begin the trip at Houston and then proceed along a normal route to Los Angeles and San Francisco. Instead, standard procedure was to suffer for a few nights in the winds of Candlestick Park, double back to Houston to experience the delights of the Astrodome and then return West to Los Angeles, as drained by adversity as the schedule makers could possibly contrive. This ploy helped the Dodgers fatten on tired Eastern teams. In 1969, when the league was split into divisions, our two Western swings took us, in illogical order, to San Diego, San Francisco and, finally, Los Angeles. Since the flights were short, the irrational doubling back could not have helped O'Malley much, except psychologically.

An additional sample of their willingness to pollute the sport is the owners' cheerful attitude toward hoodlum behavior in the bleachers and grandstands. During 1969, the Chicago Cubs actively encouraged an obscene gang of drunks known as "The Bleacher Bums." They were suitably named. Tanked to the scuppers and thoroughly inflated by the publicity they were getting, these idiots pelted visiting players with groceries, flashlight batteries and vocal abuse. My back hurt for days after a battery hit me. Mudcat Grant caught a hard rubber handball full in the face. Each time I took my position in center field I was saluted with brays of "black bastard" and "faggot."

One afternoon, Lou Brock and I both rushed to the same part of the Chicago outfield wall, trying to catch a long drive. The ball went out for a home run. At that instant,

Brock and I were trying to avoid (a) collision with each
other and (b) collision with Mr. Wrigley's vine-covered
bricks. Adding to these hazards, one of the bums poured
his beer in our faces. Only luck saved us from serious injury.

If the raucous manager of the Cubs, Leo Durocher, had
not frazzled the nerves of his own team during the latter
stages of the season, Chicago might have won the pennant
and Durocher would have been crowned manager of the
year. But a special Integrity-of-the-Game award would
have been owed to The Bleacher Bums for hazing the Cubs'
opponents.

Mention of Durocher brings us back to the subject of
field managers, the renowned personalities on whom success or failure allegedly depends. As I have pointed out,
fable portrays the manager as a unique blend of teacher,
confessor, house mother and, of course, master tactician.
Nothing could be further from the truth. Baseball's employer-employee relations are not organized that way. In
their choices of managers, and in the demands they make
of them, the proprietors derive lasting satisfaction only
from subserviently obedient organization men—men willing to agree that the Good of the Game is not necessarily
synonymous with the good of the game, but is more important.

To become managers, many players are perfectly willing
to alter their views of baseball truth, terminate long-standing social relationships with other players, and act as trained
seals for the front office. But it is not as easy as all that.
First of all, the owners tend to be suspicious of men who
convert to the only true faith, the establishment faith,
after years of behaving like ball players. First preference is
given to men who have had the foresight to curry favor
with the front office long before their playing days are over.

Among candidates who qualify on that vital score, the job goes to whomever conforms with the desired Image of the Game. Preferably he is popular with the local customers, or at least is preceded by a reputation as a stern competitor. I have already remarked that nobody can be a successful baseball player unless he is a good competitor. To acquire a public reputation as a "hustler"—a good competitor—is usually a matter of posture or personality, abetted as often as not by a penchant for making noise (a "holler guy")—or harassing umpires. Slowness of foot also helps, requiring the player to fling himself to the turf in vain efforts to catch balls that more gifted athletes might have handled while remaining unruffled and erect. The toughest battler I know is Bob Gibson. He pitches shutouts when his arm is killing him. He never shows pain. He never shows off. He has the stuff to lead men. Colored but not "colorful," he will not become a manager.

You may notice that I have not mentioned brains. From the point of view of the player, whose chief vocational interests are winning games and making more money, intelligence would be a great thing in a manager. So would the human sensitivity that sometimes accompanies intelligence. Nevertheless, the owners place no great premium on these attributes when choosing field leaders. As an arm of the front office, an executor of its policy and a barometer of its moods, the manager apparently need be no brighter than is necessary to recognize the side on which his bread is buttered. Some mighty dim people have become quite successful managers.

The leader of a pennant-winning team returned in distress from a movie called *The Vikings*, in which much gore was spilled.

"Jeez," he mused, "I'm sure glad I don't live in them days."

I include that patronizing anecdote because it indicates that a man can manage a team of high-strung athletes to a pennant while building a legend as a mental defective. Face it. Baseball is an uncomplicated game. Strategic and tactical alternatives are few. Success depends not on superb strategy, which does not exist, but on the ability of pitchers to pitch and of other players to bat, run, catch and throw. Granted, some mentalities run into tactical trouble because of inability to think two moves ahead. Yet more than one such plodder has been successful, simply because he had crack performers on his team. More serious troubles arise if the manager is too dull to play the right men at the right time. When the front office wakes up, such a helmsman gets his pink slip.

Most teams profess to spend not less than $1 million a year on so-called player development—the scouting of new talent and the support of minor-league farm clubs. Possibly some youngsters learn by instruction as well as by experience during their minor-league seasoning. But I doubt that many do. I recall no effective instruction during my two years in the minors, except when Johnny Temple was assigned the thankless task of converting me into a second baseman. I do remember that I was in dire need of coaching when I finally came up with the Cardinals. It was hard to come by. The teams are simply not organized for that purpose. The rookie either makes it in the big time or he does not. If he does not, the fault is assumed to be his. The loss is, of course, not only his but baseball's.

Despite the tedious fiction about the perspicacity of grizzled old managers and coaches, few examples have been recorded of instruction bringing success to players who might otherwise have failed. Johnny Sain, a pitching coach constantly at war with his employers because of his player-oriented outlook, has helped every pitcher with whom he has ever worked. Neither front offices nor field managers care for his insistence on husbanding a pitcher's strength (and prolonging a pitcher's career, I might add). Accordingly, the best pitching coach in baseball was without a job in baseball when this was written. Ted Williams, an original thinker and, as such, as untypical choice as a field manager, is said to have improved the batting of a few members of the Washington Senators. Wally Moses is reputed to be an effective batting coach. Harry Walker, a fanatic about batting technique, made a league-leading hitter of Matty Alou, but has talked himself blue in the face without, so far as I know, approaching that achievement with any other player. Paul Richards, a former catcher who managed for eleven years and once finished as high as second, taught all his pitchers an off-speed delivery known as the slip pitch. Not everyone thinks as much of the slip pitch as Richards does. Not everyone thinks as much of Richards as Richards does. Rube Walker may have hastened the development of the remarkable young pitchers who won the 1969 World Series for the New York Mets, although you could not get everybody to agree. Leo Durocher had sense enough to bolster the uncertain morale of the young Willie Mays, taking a fatherly interest. No doubt, dozens of similar examples of managerial or coaching acumen might be supplied, but not by me. I have told all I know. Considering the thousands of players with whom I have discussed baseball during my twelve years in the National League, it may be fair to conclude that effective instruction is unusual, and considerate personal counsel rarer still.

Batting and pitching coaches are an entertaining lot. The typical pitching coach wrinkles his brow in a display of reflection and advises the pitcher, "Bend your back and come over the top." He then stands there, hoping for the best, his fund of theory all but expended. The batting coach posts himself behind the cage and says something about rolling the wrist, shortening the stride or rotating the hips. If you hit the ball, he yells in triumph, "That's it! That's it! Now you got it!"

My own problem had to do with the bat. Having been something of a power hitter on the Oakland sandlots and, despite my size, having knocked twenty-nine balls out of the park during my first season in the minors, I had fallen into the disastrous habit of overswinging. Worse, I had developed a hitch in my swing. When the pitcher released the ball my bat was not ready, because I was busy pulling it back in a kind of windup. Birdie Tebbetts, manager of the Cincinnati Reds, noticed this in me and did not like it. In an interview some years later, after I began knocking the cover off the ball for the Cardinals, he mentioned the hitch in my swing as a reason why he had not regretted trading me. He seemed pleased that I had worked my way out of the habit. I was entertained by his tacit assumption that I had improved my own batting, without tutelage. The Reds had made no great attempt to help me, as he well knew, and the traditions of the industry did not suggest that the Cardinals or any other team would try any harder. If I did not make the bigs, somebody else would.

By the time I got to the Cardinals, I had heard often enough about my dubious batting style but was convinced neither that the flaws existed nor that I was under any compulsion to correct them if they did exist. In fifteen games at Omaha at the beginning of the 1958 season, I had batted .340 against the best minor-league pitching in the country and, on the recommendation of my manager, Johnny Keane, had been called up to the Cardinals. I batted only .261 during that season, but that was pretty good for a little rookie—not nearly bad enough to convince same that something was amiss.

During 1959, for reasons to which I shall come in a short while, I was playing in fewer games and having trouble batting above .250. I now became more worried about my swing, and more receptive to help. The coaches were willing to coach, but were not good enough theoreticians or communicators to do me much good. As usually happens when a player needs assistance of that kind, I finally got it from another player—George Crowe, who knew more batting theory and was more articulate about it than anyone else on the Cardinals. He is now selling insurance in San Francisco because baseball has no place for him. Even if he were white, I doubt that anybody would want him. Bright people tend to rock boats, or to be suspected of it. In any event, they discomfort the dull-normals in the front office.

George straightened me out. He taught me to shorten my stride and my swing, to eliminate the hitch, to keep my head still and my stroke level. He not only told me what to do, but why to do it and how to do it. He worked with me by the hour. So did Terry Moore, who then was coaching with the Cardinals. Stan Musial also helped—mainly by working as hard as he did on his own perfect swing. If this immortal felt the need for frequent extra practice, how could I hope to prosper on less effort? He was an awesome sight in the batting cage, sweat pouring, brows knit in concentration, telling the pitcher what to throw next, hammering twenty or thirty balls to the fences and beyond—polishing, polishing, polishing.

I once plucked at his sleeve for advice. I had become overanxious about the curve ball and was swinging at it too soon. When balls are being fired toward your head at ninety or a hundred miles an hour, there is no time for deliberation. I mean, you do not just *decide* to delay your bat in case the pitch turns out to be a curve. Proper timing is an end product of a properly balanced stance, a properly

hinged swing and, of course, athletic reflexes. I asked
Musial if he could tell me how to adjust my swing. He
thought for a while and then confided with total sincerity,
"Well, you wait for a strike. Then you knock the shit out
of it." I might as well have asked a nightingale how to trill.

Considering baseball standards of managerial compe-
tence, Musial would have made an adequate field manager.
That he was more doer than thinker would not have handi-
capped him in his relations with employer or players. From
the viewpoint of the front office, he met the indispensable
requirement: undeviating acceptance of the *status quo*.
Moreover, he was the most popular figure in the history of
St. Louis baseball and enjoyed cordial, even festive relations
with the press. Because he was an unpretentious man, he
would have been liked by his players. He would not have
posed as a genius, would not have demeaned his men by
accepting credit for their accomplishments. He would not
have overmanaged. He would have accepted what guidance
he required from those of his coaches and players who were
good tacticians. I am sorry that he did not want to become
a field manager. He would have done absolutely nothing to
prevent a good team from winning—which is more than
can be said for most.

If experienced players were asked to name the National
League manager whom they respected the most, I am sure
that Walter Alston of the Los Angeles Dodgers would win
hands down. He knows baseball tactics, such as they are,
and suffers from none of the intellectual or emotional
deficits that so often prevent a manager from exercising
knowledge. He wears the same face in private as on camera,
treating his players with even-tempered dignity and fairness. He never upstages anyone. The managers least likely
to win votes would be self-anointed messiahs of the type
personified by Leo Durocher and Gene Mauch. Their

gaudiness is supposed to help at the box office, but often hurts in the dugout and clubhouse. Ball players are sufficiently strung out by the tensions of the game. They don't need managerial theatrics to keep their teeth on edge. Neither do they appreciate an atmosphere in which losses are their fault (which usually is true) and victories are the manager's (which is usually false). Aware of their impermanence, ball players are easily intimidated. But as Durocher, Mauch, Eddie Stanky, and other aggressive personalities have had ample opportunity to learn, intimidated players tend to run out of gas in the homestretch.

My first manager with the Cardinals was the late Fred Hutchinson, who reacted to defeat by kicking steel lockers and swearing. The players respected him because they recognized that he was a competent judge of talent and made no unreasonable demands. In letting you know where you stood, and in doing so in private without humiliating you, he displayed more character than is customary at the managerial level. That he was no great shakes as a teacher was not held against him.

Hutchinson's successor was Solly Hemus, who deserves several paragraphs of his own and will get them. After Hemus came the late Johnny Keane, a gentle person with a competent grasp of the game but no special prowess. Like Hutchinson, Walt Alston and other superior managers, he knew who his better players were, and did not hesitate to use them in his lineup. The team liked him.

We won the National League pennant for Johnny in 1964, thanks to a late-season winning streak that coincided with the predictable collapse of Gene Mauch's enervated Philadelphia Phillies. Before this stunning turnabout (the Phillies had been far in the lead), our owner, August A. Busch, Jr., had given up on us. In the tradition of the industry, his move was to find a new manager for the next

year, much as a discontented chick might try to change her
luck with a new shade of lipstick. Having surveyed the
supply of available straw bosses, Busch settled on the noisy
Durocher, perhaps because Leo was not guilty of the incon-
spicuousness attributed to Keane.

After we won the pennant and defeated the New York
Yankees in the World Series, Busch changed his mind. He
decided that Keane was not so bad, after all. He tried to
renew John's contract. But John was not having any. God
bless him, he signed to manage the Yankees. And Bing
Devine, general manager of the Cardinals, quit to join the
New York Mets. These departures left Busch with a clutter
of Image problems. So he replaced Devine and Keane with
the two most popular baseballers he could find.

He promoted Stan Musial to the front office. As the
reader already knows, Stan's administrative gifts were not
exactly apparent while he was knocking the shit out of the
ball. But no matter. He was Stan the Man and Busch could
bolster him with whatever assistance was needed. For
field manager, Busch chose Red Schoendienst, another
popular player. Red was and is immensely personable. He
led the Cardinals to the 1967 and 1968 pennants by the
simple expedient of letting the players play. When he was
required to think two or three moves ahead, as in choosing
pinch hitters or replacing pitchers, he accepted advice
readily. And it was given matter-of-factly, with every consideration for Red's position.

"Gibson will not bat in a situation like this," a voice
would say as if in normal dugout conversation. Or, "Looks
like Briles is getting awful tired. I suppose he won't be in
there for more than two or three more pitches." Up would
go a pinch hitter for Gibson, who would return to the
bench fuming, because he loves to bat. Out would come
Briles, dog-tired. Never one embarrassingly direct word was

exchanged between the manager and his volunteer strategists. Everything worked out fine.

Under Solly Hemus, nothing worked out fine. He was manager during 1959, 1960 and half of 1961. It was common knowledge that he had obtained the job by writing a humble but hopeful letter to Mr. Busch. I have not seen the letter, but Solly once wrote one to me and I know his style. It may be assumed that he reminded Busch that he had played for the Cardinals during his prime and had always, as they say, "given 110 percent of himself." That he considered the St. Louis organization tops. That he was no recent admirer of Mr. Busch's celebrated foresight and vision. That he would like nothing more of life than an opportunity to reward Mr. Busch and the great St. Louis organization with the pennant they so richly deserved. And that it was just a matter of generating more team spirit. And that he was the one to do it. Or words to such effect.

Shades of Horatio Alger! Busch loved the letter. He all but proclaimed, "Young man, I like the cut of your jib. You're the kind of American the Cardinals need! You've got the job!"

I came to spring training camp on a cloud. My salary had been raised by 140 percent—from $5,000 to $12,000. I now was an established major leaguer, en route to the big chips. Hemus would appreciate my all-out style of play. Perhaps he would clap his hand on my shoulder and say, "Young man, I like you! Glad to have you aboard!"

Talk about disasters. Hemus did not share the rather widely held belief that I played center field approximately as well as Willie Mays. He sat me on the bench, preferring to use men such as Gino Cimoli, Don Taussig, Don Landrum and even poor Bill White, who was unquestionably the best first baseman in the league but was its most miscast outfielder. Hemus acted as if I smelled bad. He avoided my presence and when he could not do that he avoided my eye.

Having achieved the ripe old age of twenty-one, I demanded mature forbearance of myself. I tried to believe that my chance would come. All that came were insomnia and chronic indigestion. When I got into the lineup I was uneasy. Getting hits or making spectacular plays helped not a bit. I was an outcast. And I did not know why.

In a rational environment, I might have gone to Hemus and asked for a better opportunity. I might even have suggested that I could play the position better than any two of his other center fielders combined. But this was major-league baseball and I was a second-year man without an iota of bargaining strength. Stars might sometimes be able to challenge a managerial decision and win the debate, but second-year men who tried were not often around for a third year.

My roommate, Bob Gibson, was just as badly off. He could throw as hard as any man alive. He was such a fine athlete that he had moved from the Harlem Globetrotters basketball team to the Cardinals' highest minor-league farm club in 1957. Slight control problems had kept him in the minors during 1957 and 1958, but it seemed obvious that Hoot only needed work to become one of baseball's leading pitchers. Hemus did not see it that way. During 1959 and 1960 he shunted Gibson back and forth between St. Louis and the minors. He never used him if someone else was available.

"A hell of a way to treat a nice, clean-cut colored kid from Omaha," Hoot would say from his bed.

"What about me? What about a nice, clean-cut *little* colored kid from Oakland?"

"Don't change the subject."

Solly's attitude toward Hoot was evident during the clubhouse meetings that preceded each series of games.

Baseball custom required that the pitcher of the first game preside over a discussion of how each opposing batter should be handled. Like certain other rituals, these are exercises in futility. Great hitters like Henry Aaron and the Willie Mays of that era simply cannot be handled. Discussion inevitably leads to a dead end: "Don't let him hurt you. Let him have the base on balls if you have to." If the hitter under discussion is going well but is not quite an Aaron or Mays, the conclusion usually is, "Don't give him anything to hit, but don't walk him."

On the extremely rare occasion when Bob Gibson was to be the pitcher and attempted to discuss the theoretical weaknesses and strengths of opposing basemen, Hemus would interrupt contemptuously. "Don't get into fancy stuff like that, Gibson," the manager would rasp. "Just try to get the ball over the plate. If you can."

One of the tender moments of the Hemus-Gibson romance involved a Puerto Rican infielder named Julio Gotay. Like my minor-league companion, Leo Cardenas, Julio spoke little English and didn't dig the rules that forbade him to live and eat with the Caucasians at our Florida training camp. He was regarded as an eccentric, because he saved money by riding a rented bicycle from the ghetto motel to the ball park, carrying his Gelusil and Alka-Seltzer in a brown paper bag. The rest of us rode cabs or rented cars, and carried our own antacids in attache cases. Julio probably knew that he was looked upon as a screwball, but he had more important worries on his mind. For example, he had been writing home for weeks without a single reply. He managed to explain this to George Crowe. Day after day, no mail for Julio. One morning we persuaded him to leave his bike home and join us in our rented car. We stopped at a corner where he could post his communique and discovered instantly why he had been getting no answers. He hopped out, pushed back the swinging top and deposited his letter in a trash container.

I seem to have strayed from the original point. One afternoon Julio made some brilliant plays at shortstop. Later, Hemus saw Bob Gibson and said, "Wow, Julio, you did great out there today."

During a game against Pittsburgh in 1959 or 1960, Hemus inserted himself as a pinch hitter against Bennie Daniels, a black man. Daniels knocked him down with the first pitch. On the second, Solly swung, missed and let go of his bat. It flew to the pitcher's mound. Tit for tat. Nothing wrong with that. Daniels' third pitch hit Hemus in the back. As our manager trotted to first base, we saw him shouting at Daniels, but we could not hear what he was saying. Neither did we especially care.

The next day, Hemus called a team meeting in the clubhouse. "I want you to be the first to know what I said to Daniels yesterday. I called him a black son-of-a-bitch."

End of statement. End of meeting. Not one word of regret. No hint that he had perhaps acted excessively in the heat of combat. Gibson, White, Crowe and I sat with our jaws open, eyeing each other. We had been wondering how the manager really felt about us, and now we knew. Black sons-of-bitches. Any one of us could have chewed Hemus up and spit him out, but we said not a mumbling word. No white player looked at us, or mentioned the meeting afterward. We talked it over among ourselves many times and agreed that the Daniels incident had been the last straw for Hemus. The meeting had been his way of revealing the principles for which he stood. The great beliefs that prompted him to bench a good center fielder, ignore a good pitcher, and play a good first baseman out of position.

Until then, we had detested Hemus for not using his best lineup. Now we hated him for himself. We became more discerning in our evaluations of baseball's employment policies. We became connoisseurs of the Good of the Game, noting how unconcernedly the owners sabotaged the sport by hiring incompetent or prejudiced or just plain stupid managers. And we saw more clearly than before that black players of less than star quality tended to disappear from the scene in a few years, whereas mediocre whites hung on long enough to qualify for pensions: In baseball, as elsewhere, the black had to be better than a white of equal experience, or he would be shown the door.

Doubt it? During 1969, only eighteen full-time major-league players batted .300 or higher. Of these, thirteen were black. How are these statistics to be interpreted? Shall we suspect that blacks are better batsmen than whites? If so, one might expect blacks to form a majority of every major-league team, which is by no means the case. Shall we be equalitarian about it and resolve that blacks are neither better nor worse batsmen than whites? Then we might expect the batting statistics to be borne out at every level, with black players holding thirteen of every eighteen jobs.

Baseball's racism is showing. Outstanding blacks get jobs. Lesser blacks are shunted aside in favor of whites, sometimes to the detriment of a team. The mistake of Solly Hemus was not that he misused and mistreated blacks but that he overdid it.

The Horatio Alger tale ended midway through the 1961 season. Hemus departed and Johnny Keane became manager. Bob Gibson won thirteen games that year, finished fourth in the league with 166 strikeouts and fifth in earned run average with 3.24. Bill White returned to first base and batted .286 with twenty home runs. I was reinstalled in center field and ended with a batting average of .322.

According to his publicists, Mr. Busch had insisted that Keane use me. If this is true, I wish he had been more insistent when Hemus was manager. Hemus would have done anything the boss wanted. Keane, on the other hand, had always thought highly of me. His praise of my performance at Omaha had been responsible for my escape from the minors in 1958. The day he took over from Hemus, he came to me and said, "You're the center fielder, Curt."

Under Keane and Red Schoendienst, I did my thing. Only four Cardinals in history have played more games in that uniform than my 1,585, and only six have made more hits than my 1,680. I led the team in batting three times and in runs-batted-in twice. In 1963, I led the league with 662 times at bat, and hit .302. In 1964, when I batted .311, I tied Roberto Clemente of the Pittsburgh Pirates for the league lead in total hits—211. In 1967, my batting average of .335 was fourth highest in the league. In 1968 I was fifth highest with .301.

I led all the league's outfielders in putouts several times. In 1966 I set an all-time record for the majors, handling 396 chances without an error. My 226 consecutive errorless games between June 1965 and June 1967 was another record. I was on the National League all-star team three times and won the Golden Glove award for fielding every year from 1963 through 1969.

On my way to these records, feeling my oats and having a great time, I ran into Hemus in New York. We were in the old Polo Grounds, playing the Mets, who had taken him on as a coach. After a game in which I had done nicely, I was walking from our dugout to the clubhouse entrance in center field and heard a familiar voice. It was Hemus, walking in the same direction. "I never thought you'd make it in the National League," he said. I will not repeat my reply, which was lengthy and venomous, and did me a world of good.

During the 1968 World Series, I attracted unfavorable attention by missing a catch that might have been easy for me if I had not been completely bushed. Attempts were made to brand me as the Series "goat" (there must always be a hero and a goat). Lo and behold, a letter came from Solly Hemus:

Dear Curt:

After reading all of the articles in the newspapers, I *still* feel that you are one of the greatest defensive center fielders that I have seen play.

Don't let all the second-guessers upset you, because without you in the lineup, the Cardinals would not have been in the Series this year and would have missed the two previous times.

If I ever missed on evaluating a ball player it was you, and I admire you for all of your determination, guts and pride in your work.

You are not only one of the finest outfielders I have seen play, but you are a gentleman, and I admire you for this. Stay healthy and best of luck in the future. Congratulations on a fine year.

Sincerely,
Solly

I don't usually save letters, but I could not part with that one. Every time I look at it, I get sore.

5

The Winning Spirit

I do not vouch for the facts, but the story rings true. The black football star O.J. Simpson brought two friends to a cocktail rumpus in Buffalo, New York. Somebody noticed him in the crowd and exclaimed, "Look! There's O.J. Simpson with a couple of niggers!"

When I arrived on the national sporting scene, racial tokenism had not yet proceeded to its present, or cocktail-party phase. Black entertainers and athletes were accepted —even hailed—for their prowess afield or on stage, but remained outcasts between performances. If an O.J. Simpson had been invited to a white social gathering (highly unlikely) and had not been wearing a football uniform when he arrived with his friends, someone surely would have wondered who the *three* niggers were.

Having demonstrated our ability to help win ball games, and having disproved the theory that our complexions would repel white trade, we blacks seemed to have reached our absolute zenith. We were being allowed to play major-league baseball! We were being allowed to "prove" that any black kid could get ahead in this enlightened society if he would only try! What more could we possibly wish? Or, as cranky whites asked when things began to heat up in the United States during the sixties, "What do you people *want?*"

For openers, Colonel, how about eliminating skin color as a factor when you appraise another human being's worth?

"Love?" said Bob Gibson to Dwight Chapin of the *Los Angeles Times.* "No, love isn't the answer. If everybody went around loving everybody else, it would be a weird scene. Respect. That's the word. We must respect one another."

During the 1967 World Series, shortly before his interview with Chapin, Bullet Bob beat Boston three times and established himself as an all-time great. The glamor boy of the defeated Red Sox, Carl Yastrzemski, rebounded from defeat with about $200,000 worth of contracts for product endorsements and personal appearances. Gibson's testimonial glamor fetched only $2,500. Commerce had not yet conceded that blacks use razor blades, automobiles and deodorants, much less that a black's endorsement might help to sell such merchandise to whites. That Gibson had stood Yastrzemski & Co. on its ears was of no relevance. Neither was the inescapable fact that Gibson speaks more coherent and literate English than Yastrzemski and is a more impressive person. Gibson's sole problem with Madison Avenue was his blackness.

In the last couple of years, of course, institutionalized prejudice has diminished slightly. Black faces now appear in television commercials. As any frequenter of urban cocktail parties can testify, black celebrities are granted certain social indulgences.

Although genuine friendships have been established, much of this new warmth is superficial and offends us. We do not appreciate being treated as interesting exceptions by people who would never be caught under the same roof with less prominent but equally worthy blacks. This is no compliment to us as individuals. On the contrary, it supposes that we hope that our brief fame will somehow whiten us permanently. It solicits our endorsement of the false belief that (a) any worthy black can make the grade and (b) whoever is still in the ghetto deserves to be.

When Bob Gibson returned to Omaha after the 1967 Series, he had a few brushes with tokenism. He, Charline and the kids had moved into a white neighborhood a year earlier (not to invade white society but to obtain suitable housing). They had encountered the usual trouble. But now he ambled home from his World Series exploits and it dawned on the neighbors that this large nigger was a Neeegro, an authentic celebrity. Among other results of this realization, Bob was invited to join a white church. "They decided that they finally wanted one in their congregation," he told me, "and naturally they had to have a *qualified* one who gets his name in the paper and wears a sharp crease in his pants. I declined."

If I ever needed to learn that a black celebrity is first of all a black and only secondarily a celebrity, the lesson was repeatedly impressed on me during my early years with the Cardinals. One night I decided to make a big impression on a girl by taking her to a famous restaurant. I had attended one or two of the team's promotional gatherings there and looked forward to VIP treatment now that I was turning up as a paying customer—me and my .320 batting average and my unlimited charm. That girl would melt on the spot. My major problem would be persuading her to keep her cool until we got home.

The maitre d' stopped me the door.

"Can I help you?" he asked, as if wondering why I was stupid enough to make a delivery at that hour of the night, and through the front entrance to boot.

"I want a table for two," I said.

"I'm sorry," he answered without sorrow. "We don't serve you here."

Thank God I had the poise not to identify myself as Curt Flood, Baseball Star. The bastard might have given me a table.

The next day in the Cardinal clubhouse I went to Stan Musial, one of the proprietors of the famous restaurant.

"Stan, what kind of eating place are you running there?"

He looked at me. "What do you mean?"

"They stopped me at the door. I tried to take a girl to dinner last night and they wouldn't let me in."

Musial turned livid. He said he'd look into it. I never raised the topic with him again, nor did he with me. When I returned to the restaurant a few years later, St. Louis was no longer so blatant a Jim Crow town. This time the man at the door nearly piddled with joy. It was Mr. Flood this and Mr. Flood that and please let me kiss your fanny, Mr. Flood. I accepted the adulation with practiced grace, as if it were my due. I assume that I would have been treated courteously even if I had been a menial on his night out. Times had changed.

One of the funniest experiences of the early years came on a Sunday. I had overslept and needed to get to the ball park in a hurry. Had barely enough time for breakfast. Dropped into a greasy spoon along the route, climbed onto a stool at the counter and said, "I'd like some bacon, a couple of eggs over light, please, and some toast and butter."

"Bacon and eggs to go!" hollered the waitress.

"No," I said. "Not to go. I want to eat it here."

"Not here you don't," she said.

I left without ever finding out how they proposed to wrap a couple of fried eggs.

After our games, the white players went one way and we went another. My first home in St. Louis was a room in a notoriously raffish black hotel, which had been found for me by someone in the team's front office. Another resident of the place was Sam Jones, the elderly pitcher, who advised me that discontent was futile, because there was no better place for us in the whole city. I did not like sleeping on a lumpy mattress and quickly outgrew the novelty of all the lurid comings and goings in adjacent rooms. I finally found a furnished room on a quieter street, moved in and discovered that I had rented space in a whorehouse. I was the only man in residence who was not a pimp.

If I had gone to the administrative offices of the Cardinals and demanded help in finding more suitable quarters, I would have hurt my chances to stay with the team. On what possible grounds could I have justified so unusual a request? Had they not found a hotel room for me while I was en route from Omaha? What more did I want? If I had suggested that my play on the field might benefit from decent living conditions, I would have exposed myself as a crybaby, a clubhouse lawyer, an agitator, a pain in the ass. Baseball players had always found their own lodgings in the hometowns of their teams. Period. So I lived in the black whorehouse for the rest of the season.

After I became more secure in my position with the Cardinals, I suppose I did become an agitator. One of my most insistent gripes was about the segregated living conditions at our Florida training camp. The noise must have reverberated in the front office. One day, Bing Devine, the general manager, called me in and asked if I was satisfied with my accommodations.

"No," I replied.

"You have to understand that there is nothing we can do about it. Segregation is Florida law."

"Okay. Train someplace else."

"We have to be where the other teams are, so that we can play them."

"Why don't all the teams move? What's wrong with Southern California? Can't we train out there?"

"We all have big plant investments here. These things aren't easy, Curt. They take time and money."

"Shit, you've had a hundred years and money you haven't even counted."

You can only talk that way when everyone thinks you are the next Willie Mays.

In 1962 or thereabouts, segregation ended in Florida, at least as far as major-league baseball teams were concerned. We now were permitted to live in the same hotels as the other players. No more Jim Crow taxis from ball park to black motel. Big hurrahs in restaurants and night clubs from which we had once been barred. Star treatment. It was an unsettling experience to be applauded and made much of in places where the only other blacks were the bus boys. Nevertheless we welcomed the amenities. They helped to launch each baseball season on a more wholesome footing, as if a team were really a team. But were they softening us up? Were we becoming Establishment blacks? Were we going for the scene?

Before the arrival in organized baseball of Jackie Robinson, Larry Doby, Satchel Paige, Roy Campanella and the other black pioneers, the game's lily-whiteness held down its quality. Some of the best players were segregated in Negro leagues and could not enter a major-league park without buying a ticket. After the color bar was lifted, the quality of play improved but seldom achieved its full potential. One reason for this was—and is—the quota system which keeps black employment at a regulated minimum. An additional reason was—and is—the inability of baseball executives to cope with the morale problems that arise from racial tensions.

Indifference to the feelings of players and, by extension, to the quality of the game, accounted for the installation of a Solly Hemus as manager of a team whose personnel included several blacks. Not that the Cardinals had a monopoly on insensitivity, or that Hemus was the first and only big-league manager who might politely be described as backward. For several years, the San Francisco Giants and their manager, the pious Alvin Dark, were the talk of the National League's black population.

Evaluated in terms of their individual skills, the Giants usually were the best team in baseball. Yet they never played that well. Their difficulty was partly racial (black versus white), partly national (American versus Latin) and partly just plain human (black versus black and white versus white). To impose reason, understanding and order on that unholy mess was a job for a saint, which may be why the tirelessly festive owner of the club, Horace Stoneham, picked Alvin Dark. The new manager's piety had been celebrated in the newspapers for years. If his press was to be believed, he was seldom farther than arm's length from a Bible. Not that there was anything bleak about him, wrote the reporters. No, he was as amiable and communicative a ball player as any of them had known.

In other words, he was good copy. Such talent rates high on any list of managerial qualifications, but it avails little in the dugout or on the field. Especially when some Latin-American star smolders because the club gulled him into signing away his career for a $400 bonus, whereas North American whites of lesser ability got tens of thousands of dollars.

Among Dark's master strokes was an edict forbidding the
Latin-Americans to speak Spanish on the team bus. According to Orlando Cepeda, a reliable source, the Latins
assumed that Dark suspected them of using their mother
tongue for the sole purpose of blasting him. Possible.
Equally likely, Dark may have imagined that if everybody
spoke English, the team might pull together. Needless to
say, the bus remained a Babel.

I know nothing of Dark's managerial performances since
he left the Giants. Latin and black players no longer single
him out when reviewing the horrors of the industry. He
probably has become more adept. It figures. His adeptness
had nowhere to go but up. He was dismissed after committing the unforgivable error of offending Willie Mays.
The details of the incident were disputed, but I gathered
that Dark had become dissatisfied with Willie and seemed
to imply that mentalities were low among players of
Willie's color.

Granted that piety and a cordial press are great comforts
to a manager, they do not inevitably convert his team into
one big happy family. In an era of social unrest, the manager might well be chosen among former players qualified
by intellect to deal not only with God and the press but
with the team. Dozens come to mind. To name only four,
Jackie Robinson, Bill White, Robin Roberts and George
Crowe are eminently capable of overcoming the benighted-
ness and confusion that wreck so many clubs. Each might
have won repeated pennants with the same Giants who
won but once for Alvin Dark. And who finished second in
four consecutive seasons under Dark's successor, the club
owner's boon companion, Herman Franks.

Robinson, White and Crowe are black, of course. But
Roberts is white, smart, and a stout defender of the baseball
establishment's dearest prerogatives. If ever a player should
have been a manager, it was Robin. He did himself in,

however, by displaying a balanced concern for the welfare
of the players during his days as a leader of the Major
League Baseball Players Association.

If a serious study has ever been made of the phenomenon
known as team spirit, the findings have not circulated.
Everyone agrees that team spirit is desirable, but nobody
in authority seems able to cultivate or maintain it. The
collapses of the 1964 Phillies and 1969 Clubs and the repeated failures of the Giants are accepted as horrible examples of professional demoralization, yet nobody seems to
have learned anything from it. In the same vein, the Cardinals of 1967 and 1968 were a winning team because their
high talents were reinforced by a sense of fraternal closeness
unequaled in modern baseball. No prescription for success
was gleaned from this, either. Instead, the owner, August
A. Busch, Jr., launched the 1969 season with a spectacular
tantrum in which he publicly misrepresented the team's
attitudes toward the game, its fans and himself. He also
traded the team's most popular player, Orlando Cepeda.
On the seventh day he rested, with the team's morale
irreparably smashed. I shall return to this episode in a later
chapter. For now it might be interesting to explore the idea
of team spirit both as a generality and as it actually developed during the good years with the Cardinals.

It can be taken for granted that in seasonal competition
between two teams of roughly equal ability, victory will go
to the more spirited. That is, the team on which the players
are more compatible with each other and less bugged by
everything. Yet, a club truly superior in the physical sense
can succeed without much spirit. The New York Yankees
of the Mickey Mantle–Whitey Ford era won repeated
championships in an atmosphere as impersonal as a bank
vault. The superstars moved through life in a remote and
lofty clique of their own, and the others were spear carriers

grateful "to be young and a Yankee." The team was able to go out there and pitch its shutouts, hit its home runs, collect its pay and rest easy because nothing more was required. And when the superstars faded, the team collapsed. It lacked talent. And it lacked the spirit—or even the tradition of spirit—that makes up for it.

The New York Mets were an extraordinarily lucrative property during the days of Casey Stengel. They also were the worst team in the league. And their players were bitterly, hopelessly humiliated. It was not so much that Stengel fell asleep on the bench during games and could not always recall which pitchers and pinch hitters had been used. What galled the players was that they sensed no serious effort was being made to improve matters. For the immediate and foreseeable needs of the Mets organization in those early years, it was enough to have twenty-five carcasses in uniform, and Casey Stengel for an attraction. In one of the cleverest switches ever devised by a crafty management, a promotional campaign concentrated on praising the spirit of the customers instead of the team!

In due course, the Mets' athletic failings were repaired by the baseball law that gives the worst teams first and exclusive crack at the nation's outstanding high-school and college players. When some of the youngsters showed signs of becoming first-rate professionals, Gil Hodges was named manager and the Mets became serious. In 1969, with a large assist from the frantic Chicago Cubs, they won their first championship.

Illusion of team spirit is as good for the box office as the real thing, and is easier to achieve. So long as a team *looks* spirited, the owners seem happy enough. Being concerned more with form than substance, they prefer hustling players —the kind who never walk when they can trot and never trot when they can gallop. The dumb show of racing full tilt from the outfield to the dugout when the teams change sides is regarded as the sincerest possible sign of competitive integrity. And is publicized as such. And presumably helps at the gate. So do idiotic arguments with umpires. Umpires are often wrong and know it, but can seldom change their minds and, in any event, do not lose arguments. Nevertheless, some players and managers make grand opera out of every missed call, bellowing, kicking dust at the umpire's feet and waving their arms with theatrical vehemence. These also are prized employees. They show hustle.

Alas, team spirit is something quite different. The showmanly, stereotyped hustler may or may not be a good team man. His colleagues may despise him if, like one or two famous hustlers, he races to and from the dugout, tears to first base after being walked, yet sometimes shows no enthusiasm about chasing a batted ball that has gone through his legs. His moments of immobility may go unnoticed in the grandstands, but are conspicuous on the field. They betray him for what he is—a self-seeking, self-absorbed hot dog and, as such, an unreliable competitor. As we say about such characters, "He's a real hustler. Runs out every base on balls. Looks good in the hotel lobby. Never speaks ill of the boss."

When adequately paid and housed, reasonably free of other personal problems, and permitted to go out there and do his thing, the professional baseball player behaves professionally. Unhappy players are not always capable of top effort, but they usually try. They try because it is in the professional tradition to do so, and because next year's salary reflects this year's performance, and because most men have pride.

I remember Orlando Cepeda playing daily with a case of influenza so severe that he could scarcely hold his head up.

"Orlando, goddamnit, you've got to take a couple of days off. You're going to kill yourself. You'll get pneumonia."

He looked at me blearily and said, "I don't want them to think I'm jaking."

Players willingly endure pain and risk permanent injury rather than be accused of "jaking." You are supposed to play until you drop.

Cepeda had been traded to us with a reputation as a troublemaker. He had been indispensable to our 1967 championship, when he batted in 111 runs and also supplied a personal exuberance that we had lacked. He was our cheerleader, our glue. And there he sat with a fever, worrying that the front office might think he lacked spirit.

In 1969, my old friend Vada Pinson came to the Cardinals. He was still a great ball player when he arrived, but was in grave straits before the season ended. He had played for two weeks on a broken leg. The pain was fearful, but neither the team trainer nor its physician could find anything wrong. So he played, rather than be a jaker. I finally persuaded him to get an X-ray, which revealed the broken bone and torn tissue. He wore a cast for two weeks, came out of it limping and was traded to Cleveland during the winter. I was happy to read that he was batting well during the 1970 season. Maybe he had recovered.

I've gone in for some of those heroics myself. Early in my Cardinal career, when I knew that eight or ten guys were lurking in the minor leagues, ready to take my job away, a pitched ball left me with a compound fracture of the little finger on my right hand. They delayed the game for fifteen minutes while our trainer pulled the ruin back into shape and taped it up. In the ninth inning, with the score tied, I came to bat again and hit the winning home run, just as in the storybooks. I then went to the ambulance. At the hospital they stitched up the finger and put it into a plastic splint. I played the next game. No jaker, this kid.

In 1969, a similar incident helped to expedite my de-

parture from the Cardinals. Rather than seem vulnerable
to pain, I had played with a deep gash in my right thigh,
incurred when Bud Harrelson of the Mets accidentally
spiked me in a collision at second base. What with the
stitches, the tetanus shot and general wear and tear, I had
a sore and sleepless night. I finally corked off in the morning and missed the team's most emphasized promotional
banquet of the season. No offense is less forgivable than
that. For my arrogant and thoughtless failure to awaken in
time, drag my torn self to the banquet and pay tribute to
season-ticket holders galore, I was fined $250. I protested
angrily. I protested more things than one during that horrible season. Each complaint became another nail in my
coffin. I was not speaking well of the boss. At $90,000 a
year, I no longer looked so good in a hotel lobby. My days
were numbered.

The 1969 Cardinals were a sorrowful and embittered
group, and showed it on the field. But the Cardinals of
1967 and 1968 must have been the most remarkable team
in the history of baseball. I speak now of the team's social
achievements, without which its pitching, batting and fielding would have been less triumphant than they were. The
men of that team were as close to being free of racist poison
as a diverse group of twentieth-century Americans could
possibly be. Few of them had been that way when they
came to the Cardinals. But they changed.

We murdered the National League in 1967 and 1968
because we were the best, and knew it. We were so much
the best that we might have won even if we had felt no
particular regard for each other. We might have won even
if we had feared and hated the manager. We might have
won even if we had been discontented about our pay, our
living and traveling conditions, and the personnel policies
of the front office. Other teams had overcome such handi-

caps through the simple exercise of professional pride and
championship skill. We could have done the same. For-
tunately, we did not have to. Within the traditional limits
of baseball's employer-employee relations, ours was a relatively generous organization. Our salaries compared more
than favorably with those of other teams. We traveled
more comfortably than most in a chartered jet and stopped
at decent hotels. Our manager, Red Schoendienst, was a
friendly, unobtrusive, considerate man who did not distract
us from our jobs. All this was fine. It helped us to win in
1967 and 1968. But our unique spirit guaranteed those
pennants. It would have won them for us against any team
I have ever seen.

I say that confidently, because I have never seen a team
more talented than ours was. And I have never heard of a
team whose spirit approached ours. I am proud of this
for all the obvious reasons, plus one that should be spelled
out: The initiative in building that spirit came from black
members of the team. Especially Bob Gibson.

It began where motivation always begins in baseball. We
wanted to win championships so that we could make more
money. And we blacks wanted life to be more pleasant,
championships or not. The process took five or six years.
It began with Gibson and me deliberately kicking over
traditional barriers to establish communication with the
palefaces.

"How about coming out for a drink after the game?"
Hoot would ask a player who had never gone to a bar with
a black man in his life. He was turned down more than
once. So was I. But the spirit was infectious. After breaking
bread and pouring a few with us, the others felt better
about themselves and us. Actual friendships developed.
Tim McCarver was a rugged white kid from Tennessee
and we were black, black cats. The gulf was wide and deep.

It did not belong there, yet there it was. We bridged it. Without imposing blackness on Tim or whiteness on ourselves, we simply insisted on knowing him and on being known in return. The strangeness vanished. Friendship was more natural and normal than camping on opposite sides of a divide which none of us had created and from which none of us could benefit.

Friendship was better for the team. It brought that World Series loot closer. It was a more potent force than the locker-room pranks and other forms of on-the-job congeniality which had previously been the limits of baseball togetherness. We knew each other's families. Those of us with a taste for the joys of the night swapped booze and chicks from one end of the country to the other. "The team that sins together wins together," said a motto on our clubhouse bulletin board. Also, "The team that lays together stays together." And Tim McCarver thoughtfully posted one in the bathroom: "The team that shits together hits together."

Juvenile? For a certainty. It was baseball, and not to be confused with the National Academy of Sciences. However, it was baseball at a new level. Nobody on that team had occasion to utter the usual petty platitude, "I don't care if he's white, black, purple or green, just so he does his job on the field." On that team we cared about each other and shared with each other and, face it, inspired each other. As friends, we had become solicitous of each other's ailments and eccentricities, proud of each other's strengths. We had achieved a closeness impossible by other means.

And we did it all by ourselves. When the front office appointed Tim McCarver and me the co-captains of the team, it acknowledged a reality that had developed without its prior assistance or even, so far as we could tell, its prior awareness. Front offices do not traffic in abstractions.

Daily readers of the sporting pages will please note that we developed our beautiful unity on a club that included several players with unpromising reputations—if a man's reputation be whatever is said of him in the sporting pages. Orlando Cepeda had been traded to us by San Francisco after becoming known there as a prima donna. Too much "Latin temperament" or something, the official version went. The fact of course was that Cha-Cha had been half out of his tree with frustration over the intellectual and spiritual meanness of the Giants and, beyond that, the unforgivable baseball they played. Welcomed into baseball's first genuinely civilized atmosphere, he responded with high spirit, selfless professionalism and tremendous batting power.

Roger Maris was another. In 1961 he had hit sixty-one home runs for the New York Yankees, breaking Babe Ruth's record. Instead of being lionized, he was represented to the public as an egocentric grouch. Anyone with the dimmest curiosity or sensitivity might have been able to understand Roger's frame of mind during that pressure cooker of a year. But those qualities were in short supply, and Rog came off with an almost uniformly bad press. His problem had been one of trying to maintain personal equilibrium—including his powers of athletic concentration—while being hounded by reporters and fans. To rebuff one reporter was enough to launch chain reactions of outrage. To accommodate all fans and all reporters was physically and mentally impossible. As he approached Ruth's record, the pressures became more severe, and the fans and reporters became more numerous, more insistent and touchier. He could not handle it. He never hit more than thirty-three home runs in any season after 1961. I think he was psychologically incapable of exposing himself to another ride on that particular merry-go-round.

We were apprehensive about him when he joined us in 1967. Would he fit in? Or would he sulk in his corner and cast a pall, as he supposedly had done with the Yankees? He turned out to be a great guy. He loved the Cardinal atmosphere. He joined our revels with great enthusiasm and, although he was a hard-used thirty-three years old, hampered by the after-effects of many injuries, he was as instrumental as anyone in our victories of 1967 and 1968.

Another human porcupine, if you believed his press notices, was Bob Gibson. Not only was he supposed to be a supermilitant black, but it seemed that he enjoyed making other people uncomfortable about it. The truth was that Bob tolerated no racist garbage. But I think that my story already has shown that he was more interested in ending racial estrangement than accentuating it. I can't think of any Cardinal who did not honor him for his dignity.

And so there we were, including the volatile Cepeda, the impossible Maris and the impenetrable Gibson—three celebrated non-candidates for togetherness. There we were, Latins, blacks, liberal whites and redeemed peckerwoods, the best team in the game and the most exultant. Victorious on the field and victorious off it, by God. A beautiful little foretaste of what life will be like when Americans finally unshackle themselves.

If any hint of the team's interracial closeness was reported in the daily press, I never saw the clipping. Mention may have been made of our superstitious dependence on the strength-giving properties of tomato-rice soup. And of our ritual insistence on using a half-red, half-white ball for infield practice. Sophomoric high-jinks of that kind are standard in baseball, great fun and accepted as the hallmarks of team spirit. That our brand of spirit was rooted in something more profound would have made good copy, of course, but we did not go around discussing it with newsmen. Close relations are rare between ball players and the reporters who travel with the team. The chief reason is that the players fear the daily press. They are conditioned by experience to assume that its power is likely to be used against them. They regard the typical baseball reporter as an agent of the team's front office.

This belief is not always without foundation. Just as the owners of the national pastime managed to exempt themselves from the burdens of the normal, equitable employer-employee relations prescribed by our laws, they also won exemptions from most of the Fourth Estate. By and large, the function of the baseball writer is less journalistic than promotional. His traveling expenses, hotel rooms, food and frolic are as likely to be underwritten by the club as by the newspaper that employs him.

None of this escapes the attention of the players. They notice how hesitant most reporters are to reveal the nitty-gritty fundamentals of baseball economics and baseball politics. They observe how the front office uses the sporting page as a bargaining instrument, releasing statements (often attributed to unnamed sources), that diminish the player's power to wangle better contracts for himself. This effect is achieved by the merest hint that all is not well with the player's personality, his relationship with management, his attitude, his stamina, his arm, his glove or his batting eye. Which is why so many naturally sociable players become surly or secretive when the writer walks through the club-house door.

Until I filed suit against baseball's exemption from the antitrust laws, I had no particular difficulty with baseball reporters. Like most players, I was showman enough to offer amiable and innocuous answers to routine and predictable questions. Besides, some of them never spoke to me. Of these abstainers, the most amusing was Bob Burnes, columnist for the *St. Louis Globe-Democrat*, who also conducts a popular sports program on radio. In airing his distress about my lawsuit, Burnes conveyed the distinct impression that he knew me inside and out. The truth was that he had not interviewed me once during my twelve years with the team. Matter of fact, he seldom came into the clubhouse at all, apparently having developed more efficient and less fatiguing methods for collecting information.

Burnes' printed and broadcast version of me and my litigation irritated me. To scratch back, I got someone to telephone him during the question-and-answer period of his radio program. Why, asked my friend, had Burnes never interviewed Curt Flood in all those twelve years? I wish I had taped the answer, which was not a model of candor. In effect, Burnes said that there had been sort of a communications gap and that I had not been available to interviewers. Ha!

I remember one occasion on which I and his other baseball-playing admirers were available in force. The team had been ordered to gather in the clubhouse for an important message. The message bearer turned out to be Burnes, in his role as a P.R. worker for the United Fund, of which none other than August A. Busch, Jr., was publicity chairman. We players did not enjoy Busch's efforts to impress us with our philanthropic responsibilities. We figured that he should give his Fair Share to the United Fund, if he chose, but should not try to eke it out with contributions from us. I mean, I wasn't putting Aunts and Uncles brochures in *his* pay envelope, was I?

At any rate, there stood Burnes rather nervously. All season long he had been razzing the bejeezus out of players in his column, and now he was asking us for a contribution to the boss's favorite charity. Busch would have been better off if he had sent Hitler. Having elicited no cheers, Burnes left in a hurry. We had dead-panned him out of there.

Another type of journalism was practiced by the team's famous television and radio play-by-play broadcaster, Harry Caray. Most of us liked him personally, because he was a convivial companion, but his rabble-rousing descriptions of ball games made our flesh crawl. His specialty was enthusiasm for the Cardinals as an institution, tempered with harsh objectivity toward the individual player's performance. Because he, too, was a Cardinal employee, his detachment never extended to the executive tier of the firm. That is, he "called 'em as he saw 'em," but he was careful to see nothing that the front office didn't want him to see.

"Here comes Dal Maxvill with a chance to win it for the Cardinals in the ninth," Harry would gargle in a voice that sounded as if a peanut butter sandwich had stuck in his throat. "Maxvill is hitless in his last fourteen at-bats. Koufax is ready. Here's the pitch. OH NO! HE *POPPED IT UP!* Oh, no!"

When he cried "Oh, no" as he often did, Harry was signaling his millions of loyal listeners that he and they had been bilked. How long could they be expected to endure such treatment at the hands of a Dal Maxvill?

Harry's judgments were influential, both immediately and cumulatively. By affecting public opinion, he affected our livelihood. So we kept tabs on his broadcasts. If our stock was going down, we needed to know it. Whoever among our pitchers was not working on a particular day was sure to be in the clubhouse, listening to Harry's spiel.

I still have a tape of his broadcast from Chicago on the day I made a leaping catch so improbable that a photograph of it wound up on the cover of *Sports Illustrated*. I cherish the tape for that reason, but also for a typical Carayism that occurred earlier in the inning. I had retrieved a batted ball and thrown it back to the infield. Enemy base runners were in full flight, the crowd was screaming and so was Harry: "Oh no! Flood missed the cut-off man again!" *Again!*

If baseball players seem hypersensitive about such things, it is because they have damned good reason. In a freer market, they might well adopt the attitude of other entertainers: "I don't care what he says, so long as he spells my name right." But their individual bargaining power now is so feeble that they overreact to all public criticism, deserved or not.

After a quarter-century of faithful and effective service to the club, Harry left St. Louis abruptly and became a play-by-play broadcaster in Oakland. The explanations for his change of venue included hints of intrigue. Some wise guy celebrated the event with an Oriental epigram:

> *Broadcaster who antagonize wrong woman*
> *Commit Harry Caray*

We Cardinals of 1967 and 1968 loved what we had accomplished in baseball. It seemed to us that we were the greatest bunch of human beings on earth. In conversations with players on other teams, we were positively evangelical in describing what we had. We were the envy of the league not only because we were the best team but because we were the warmest and closest.

Breaking with the rickety traditions of the sport, we went out of our way to make new players feel at home. In my own first, nervous days at the Cincinnati training camp, my locker adjoined that of the mighty Ted Kluszewski, who behaved as if I did not exist. This smart-ass upstaging of rookies was intended to make it tougher for them to take the jobs of older men. On the Cardinals, we saw each newcomer as the man whose confidence, if unimpaired, might get us into a World Series. We did everything we could to help him.

One particularly bashful rookie was a pitcher named Ron Willis. His strongest epithet was "darn." He looked as if he belonged in high school. We fussed over him and encouraged him and kidded him. One day he showed that he had become a member of the club. Nellie Briles had lost a game when somebody on the other team hit a fantastically long home run off him. In the clubhouse, young Ron asked Nellie, "Would you mind showing me how you hold your fast ball? I have never seen anyone throw a fast ball that far."

Steve Carlton, a left-hander with enormous talent, was always certain that each inning would be his last. "I haven't got it," he would moan to me on the bench while our side was at bat. "I'm shot. I'll never make it. They better take me out."

I used to give him the old Knute Rockne. "Goddamnit, Carlton, you gotta hang in there. You're all we've got. Now get your ass in gear and earn your money." And he would drag his miserable self to the mound and throw the best left-handed stuff since Koufax, dying with every pitch.

Like most pitchers, his concentration was so intense that it took him a while to return to reality after a game. After losing a close one in the ninth inning, poor Steve was hauled before a KMOX microphone for a live interview with Harry Caray. He was not yet with it. "What did he hit off you?" asked Caray. Steve tried to collect himself, but didn't make it all the way. "Fast ball, about cock high," he blurted. It went out over the air and made him our hero of the week.

The concentration process began for Bob Gibson on the day before the game, when he would withdraw to his own innermost recesses and snarl at anyone who disturbed him. During the game itself, he was at us constantly. "Get me some runs, you miserable bastards," he would mutter in the dugout. And, as the game proceeded, he'd begin moaning, "I'm just a poor, clean-cut colored kid. Can't you help me out with just one run? One run! Is that too much for you mothers to do?"

When we finally put a run together, I'd say, "Okay, Bullet Bob! We got you the run! The rest is up to you, baby! You're on your own!"

Lord, it was a feast. At the end of each clubhouse meeting, Red Schoendienst reminded us that we needed proper rest at night and that good players run to first base as fast as they can after hitting the ball. "Run everything out and be in by twelve," he would say, compressing his advice into one short sentence. Gibson gave it a twist that became a team motto: "Run everything in and be out by twelve." No unkindness was intended. We respected Red's decency. He had no pretensions. He never tried to play genius. He ran everything out and was in by twelve.

Only one player failed to respond positively to the climate of that ball club. Alex Johnson, a black outfielder, looked like Hall of Fame material when he came to us in 1966 after a promising year with the Phillies. He was big, fast, strong and beautifully coordinated. He could hit the ball out of sight. He was unsociable, his sovereign right, but he carried it onto the field with him. What appeared to be walled-off concentration turned out in the heat of battle to be daydreaming, or something undiagnosable. "Hey, Alex!" I would yell after he had endangered our World Series swag by throwing to the wrong base or missing a signal. "Hey! Don't screw up my ten thousand bucks!" We never could get a rise out of him.

One afternoon, Stan Musial, Marty Marion, Joe Medwick and I went to the ball park several hours ahead of time, having arranged to meet Alex and help him with his hitting. He did not show up until five o'clock, too late to do anything.

"I forgot," he said.

I was beside myself. "Alex, you ought to find something to do that you like better than baseball." I meant it. He just shrugged. During our big 1967 season, he did very little for us. He simply was there, distant as ever. When one of the World Series games at Boston developed into a ticklish thing, Red decided to use a pinch hitter. He called for Johnson. Alex was nowhere to be seen. We finally found him in the clubhouse, eating a sandwich. He did not play in the Series at all. In 1968 he went to Cincinnati, where he had a couple of good years before being sent to the American League. The other day I read that he has been knocking the cover off the ball for the California Angels. The team apparently had solved the Johnson problem by letting him be himself. That would seem to have been the right approach, but we Cardinals were so together that we couldn't leave anyone alone.

So we did not infect Alex Johnson with our good fellow-ship, our abolition of racial mistrust, our resultant freedom to concentrate on winning baseball games. Nor did we jiggle the brains in the Cardinals' administrative branch. Until the winter of 1969–70, by which time the team had been dismantled and the whole, beautiful thing was over with, the Cardinals employed no Negro in the front office. During that winter, they hired Johnny Lewis to present his pleasant black face as a token at promotional functions. But Johnny was a former ball player. When it came to penetrating the business structure we blacks never made it. A couple of years earlier, it had occurred to the office that it might be nice to have a pretty "one" as a receptionist. Somebody asked Lou Brock if he knew "one." He came up with a fantastic-looking chick who had a good secretarial job in private industry. The brass were unwilling to match her salary, let alone give her a pay raise to make the move attractive. And that was the end of all of it.

6

The National Pastime's Pastime

Beneath its clutter of unanswered mail, the ball player's attache case contains a portable dispensary of chemicals for the relief of his occupational discomforts. Aspirin for his headaches. Antacids. Laxatives. Elixirs to pacify the irritable colon. Salve for the hemorrhoids with which stress and strain festoon the big-league butt. Potions for sleeplessness. Tranquilizers for especially hairy days. Pep pills to transform the tranquilized into a competitive tiger.

Girls are more therapeutic. They are more fundamental. The ball player uses them medicinally, like an apple a day. They divert his mind from the panic and uncertainty of his profession. They quiet the yips with which his nervous system rewards him for his efforts on the field. They do this by comforting his flesh in the privacy of their own. They are the ultimate remedy.

Furthermore, he likes sex. As a young, vigorous stud with a normal allotment of hormones, he likes sex very much. In this respect, he differs not at all from young men in more sedentary or less public occupations. No, the differences lie in the abundance of women eager to accommodate his needs because of what he is, or what he represents, and most particularly because of their own playful appetites.

If promiscuity is hit-and-run sex without emotional involvement, the baseball player wears the badge. Yet he is as discriminating as a rajah. The girl must be attractive enough to occasion no embarrassment in public places, should they ever chance to be in one. She must lay promptly, enthusiastically and expertly, without unreasonable demands for repartee, gratitude, financial consideration or time. Especially time. He has so little of it. He needs his sleep and takes unkindly to female chatter after the mission has been accomplished. If she wants to go home, she is perfectly capable of getting there herself.

Nor can the player afford to hang around night spots, consuming alcohol while awaiting the pleasure of some chick. Baseball is played with hangovers, but not consistently well. The average player—as well as the star—is disciplined not to jeopardize his career with too much sauce. I know a superstar who spikes his beer with double bourbons and performs erratically. I have known a few dozen other players for whom the sport became a way station to abject alcoholism. Each man finds his own route to wretchedness, I suppose. But baseball players generally are more interested in pennants and copulation than in alcohol, a formidable antagonist of both.

At any given time during the baseball season, at least 360 major-league baseball players, managers, coaches and other glamorously uniformed types are away from home. Of these, at least 300 are as randy as minks, a condition which becomes chronic in their earliest minor-league seasons, when they discover that no player need suffer sexual deprivation. In whatever stadiums baseball is played, and wherever the players sleep, eat or socialize, avid women swarm. Talk about the balance of nature!

The lower the minor league, the smaller the towns, the more furtive the sex. Also, the babes are fewer and more disheveled. As a black in two peckerwood bush leagues, I missed out on the traditional gang bangs in the back seats of cars, on the shores of lakes and in tourist cabins. I did not grieve. The towns were full of girls eager to see what it was *really* like, and whether the rumors were true.

When I arrived in the majors, front offices were edgy about black players conversing in public with the white chicks who chased them. I understand that more than one cat was exiled to the minors for defending his right to associate with any consenting female he chose. All this passed rather quickly. Those most protective of the Image of the Game may have realized that it was impolitic to make a big issue of who was screwing whom. Not with adultery as rampant and widespread as it always had been in major-league life.

Among the high points of each recent Cardinal season were the great parties we threw for ourselves on the road. The financing came from our private kangaroo court— trivial fines paid to Mike Shannon for errors or omissions on the playing field. We'd pick a day on which no game was scheduled, rent half a motel in a town like Atlanta, buy enough food and drink for a brigade, gather around the pool and swing ourselves simple. The manager and coaches were barred, to spare them the assaults of conscience to which they might have been susceptible if they concurred in a breach of training rules. Inasmuch as we were away from home and continence was abhorrent to most of us, we were forced to recruit female companionship. In case any baseball wife boggles at this, let her rest assured that her own husband was never involved. We admired and respected his sobriety and his ministerial rectitude. He was an inspiration to us all. So were his closest friends on the club. None of them ever had any fun.

Which reminds me of the prominent journalist who had an insatiable yearning for black babes. One night he came into a predominantly black spot in Hollywood, saw me at a table, sat down, went through the amenities and finally zeroed in. "Do you happen to know a fine, swinging chick who might like to have a fine, swinging time with me?"

"No sooner said than done!" I trotted off to the phone.

About half an hour later, the girl arrived. She was a tall, busty Scandinavian, decked out in mink and diamonds and overjoyed by the chance to meet the great man. When she finally went to the powder room, he looked at me uncomfortably and said, "Hell, Curt, don't you know a *black* girl?"

"You ought to be ashamed! Why would you suggest a thing like that? Just because I'm colored?"

He may have guessed that I was putting him on, but he'll never be certain.

The baseball establishment is permissive about revelry. Its watchword is discretion. A player besmirches the Image of the Game if he is seen abroad after midnight. The public expects him to get his beddy-bye. But if he spends those same hours frolicking in his hotel room with two tarts, because he is unobserved the Image of the Game remains untainted.

The front office becomes exercised about the team's leisure pastimes when its competitive performances fall below par. The Giants once had locks installed on the telephone dials in the players' hotel rooms. Other teams resort intermittently to bed checks—attempts to guarantee that each player will sack in on time. On the Cardinals we were required to cork off two-and-a-half hours after the team bus returned to the hotel from a night game. After day games we were supposed to be in bed at midnight.

The customary bed check is by phone. It rings. The player answers. "You there, Curt?" says a coach. "No, but I expect to be here any minute," I reply. Some players wait for the phone call and then go out. But most of us are diligent about rest—especially when the team is going badly enough to bring on the bed checks. We get our wheeling and dealing over with at a prudent hour and then go to sleep, insomnia and indigestion permitting.

When the Cardinal management suspected that some of the cats were sneaking out after the telephone checkups, they detailed coaches to knock on doors. Before the team granted its stars the privilege of private rooms on the road, I shared space with Bob Gibson, a dear companion who gets the grouch on the day before he is scheduled to pitch. At two o'clock in the morning of one of Bob's pitching days several years ago, the heavy thinkers in the front office decided to see if all the players were in. We were awakened by a rapping on our door. I opened it. There stood Dick Sisler, the coach.

"Just checking," he smiled.

Gibson flew out of bed and stuck his nose in Sisler's face. "If you ever come to our room again," he said, "you'd better be prepared for a good time. We're going to drag you in. We're going to tie you up. We're going to force liquor down your throat. We're going to get you *raped*. Is that perfectly clear?"

Awakening a high-strung pitcher to find out if he is asleep is standard baseball idiocy. One morning in Chicago, after a similar bed check, I spotted Red Schoendienst in a hotel restaurant, joined him for breakfast and attempted to hack a new path through the thickets of baseball tradition.

"You've got this idea of bed checks ass-backwards," I said with the diplomacy for which I am so justly noted. "If you think that the men aren't getting proper rest, *tell* them. Tell them, 'Tonight I'm going to check. I want every son-of-a-bitch in bed by twelve.'"

"It wouldn't work," said Red after a period of thought.

"Why not?"

"If I tell them that I'm going to check, they'll all stay home. They'll all be in there when the coaches come around!"

"Right!" I cried in triumph. "The idea is not to catch 'em out but to keep 'em in! The idea is not to fine 'em but to rest 'em!"

"Wouldn't work," said Red. I was unable to budge him. I departed in confusion, wondering if he was right and I was wrong.

When the Giants locked the telephone dials, they attended to the less important half of the instrument's double function. The outgoing call isn't the one that matters. The incoming call is the restful way to meet girls on road trips. You sit in your room and the telephone never fails to ring.

"Hello, Mr. Flood?"

"Yes, dear. Who are you?"

"Curt?"

"Yes, darling."

"Curt, you don't know me but my name is Brenda. Are you busy?"

"Brenda? What a lovely name!"

"I mean I saw you play tonight and I'm in the lobby and I wondered if you'd like me to come up for a drink."

"Why bless your heart! But can you wait half an hour or so?"

"Yes."

"Are you sure I don't know you, dear? What do you look like?"

"No, we've never met, Curt."

"Are you sure I didn't notice you in the stands at the ball park?"

"Maybe you did. I was in the fourteenth row just behind the Cardinal dugout. I have long red hair and I look a mess because I haven't been home since this morning."

"I bet you're *beautiful*. I'll come down and get you in half an hour."

Next move is to sneak down to the lobby and take a peek, or have a teammate do it. If the girl passes muster, the next phase begins. If not, you sit by the phone and wait for another applicant to call. I mean, like you have to play things by ear in this game.

The reader may wonder how in the world the girls know where to find the players. So do I. They know more about us than our front offices do. Their psychology is much like that of the "groupies" who are forever crashing the pads of rock musicians, counting each celebrity's spasm as a new feather in the cap. Still, our camp followers are less knocked-out and unstrung than some of the groupies I have seen. They dress in more conventional fashion, are not hung up on pot (which is not widely used in baseball), and tend on the whole to be presentable. They come in all sizes, shapes, colors and ages. Some are married. Many are beautiful. A few are wealthy, like Chicago Shirley, who entertains players from both major leagues not only at home but on road trips of her own.

Shirley is regarded as the game's foremost safety. That is, safety valve. When all else fails after a long, tough day, you get out the address book and begin telephoning the safeties. Some of them are nymphos, of course. It is one thing, and hygienic enough, for a woman to want a big, strong athlete. But it gets heavy when the same woman turns out to want three at a time. Short of such extremes, the safety renders pleasant service and gets the same in return. Fundamentally, she is a relaxant. She makes baseball easier.

Obviously, not all bedmates are safeties. Neither is the telephone the only medium of introduction. Sit long enough in a place like the Martinique, in St. Louis, or Mr. Laff's, in New York, and you will see an overwhelming majority of the players in both leagues. You will also see hundreds of girls. The players go to these places because the girls do. And vice versa.

A particularly elegant way to meet a new chick is at the ball park itself. There she sits in a forward row, batting her lashes at you and taking deep breaths. You grab a baseball, write your hotel telephone number on it, plus "Please call," and toss it into her pretty lap, as if it were a plain old autographed ball. It works. Sometimes it picks up a little reverse English, as I once discovered in a Chicago hotel room shortly after checking in. The hotel is used by several ball clubs. On the floor of my room I found an address book. I opened it. It read as if it were a copy of my own. It listed the usual safeties in every town, plus other girls whom I had been sure were "mine." One bird of whom I was especially fond denied outright that she knew the other player. I had met her at Wrigley Field with the autographed ball gimmick. The experience emphasized what I had known all along but had not brooded about. Traveling baseball players offer a narrow kind of sex which relatively few women enjoy. Those who do like it are true enthusiasts. So they seek us out, and when we leave town, they seek others like us.

Before discussing the painful subject of baseball marriages, a word is in order about the grand and glorious pastime known as beaver shooting. Jim Bouton created a stir in 1970 when his book, *Ball Four*, revealed the high incidence of voyeurism among ball players. I leave it to the psychologists to decide why ball players are peeping toms or, perhaps, why peeping toms are ball players. My own theory is that most men are peeping toms, especially in private or, as among ball players, where sex is on every mind. My collaborator, Richard Carter, recalls an afternoon at the bar of the National Press Club in Washington, where the members and guests were buzzing about an important State Department press conference which many of them had just covered. Suddenly the bar emptied. Everyone had rushed to the windows to stare across the street into a room at the Hotel Willard. The lower end of a bed was visible. On it was a pair of long, lissome, bare legs. The view terminated just short of what the eminent reporters and commentators agreed were undraped female parts. The audience remained glued to the windows for at least twenty minutes until the legs finally ambulated, attached to a man in a pair of boxer shorts.

Being irreversibly convinced that we should make love, not war, I regard Carter's reminiscence as the most cheering news I have heard in years about the U.S. State Department. To me, any nonviolent manifestation of sex is an expression of joy, real or potential. I am for it. I do not claim to have been the foremost beaver shooter in the history of organized baseball, but I was big league all the way. Anyone who finds something unwholesome in the activity simply lacks appreciation of female topography. I agree that obsession with peeking may tend to limit the prospects of a man, but I insist I only become preoccupied when an occasion arises.

The best beaver shooting is in the minor leagues, where wooden stadiums permit easy boring of holes in dugout roofs. The seats in closest view of the dugout peepholes are often occupied by ladies who deliberately leave their underpants at home, the better to provoke the male scurrying and scrambling and wolf whistling that add so much to their enjoyment of the game. Leaving nothing to chance, they cross and uncross their legs at frequent intervals, presenting the athletes with a splendid vista of the promised land. Sometimes, occupants of the front row prop their feet on the rail. To many aficionados, the shooting of such eager beaver is not sporting. Real buffs prefer the beaver unaware. Here again, the minor leagues are the happy hunting grounds. You usually have to walk beneath the wooden stands to get to and from the clubhouse. An occasional upward glance leads inevitably to great discovery, a congregation of noisy athletes and a stern lecture from the manager—after he has had his own full share of the view.

In large major-league ball parks, field glasses are a great help, enabling one to achieve distant shots impossible with the naked eye. Yet one can make out on 20/20 vision alone. Some of the most earnest conferences on the pitching mound have nothing to do with baseball tactics, but are convened by a sharp-eyed catcher or infielder who wishes to share a particularly fetching beaver with his colleagues.

It must be evident by now that baseball life poses a severe challenge to the durability of marriage. This would be true even if wenching were not the national pastime's national pastime. The sex life of the traveling player should be seen in perspective. It is not the root cause of marital disgruntlement, but compounds it.

To begin with, it is immensely difficult to establish and maintain a stable home life when (a) the husband is on the road for more than three months a year and (b) he never knows when a trade will require him to relocate the family. If there are children, decisions must be made about them. Is it better for the wife and kids to remain in the bungalow back in Catawba, seeing Dad on occasional flying weekends? Or should they move at great expense to the major-league city, and follow him after the inevitable midseason trade, or when he is released to a succession of bush-league towns? What of the kids' schooling?

And who are this husband and wife in the first place? Emotional maturity runs no higher among them than in other segments of the population. Indeed, the marriage may have begun on a footing more infirm than most. Perhaps the player was a high-school hero and married the cheerleader before either of them was dry behind the ears. Or maybe he got married in the minor leagues, not necessarily because he had found his true soulmate, but because he was full of his burgeoning prowess, saw nothing but glory ahead and wanted a dear little woman to share every delicious step of the way.

Let us assume that the youngsters are compatible, as many baseball couples indeed are. The chances are small that they will emerge from the typical four- or five-year major-league career with love, respect and stability intact. I do not claim that their marriage would follow a smoother course if he abandoned baseball and took a job selling bonds, teaching school or pumping gas. The national divorce rate discourages any such belief. But I think it useful to understand that in his married life, as in everything else, the baseball player is by no means as well off as the public has been told.

When the team is at home, the player lives at home. If the marriage has not been rocky and his game is going well, these home stands are the best part of his season. But if he is struggling, and brooding about it, and the wife and/or kids are on his neck, something gives. A sadly familiar sight is the player who shows up at the home park early on the afternoon of a night game, ostensibly to take extra hitting practice but actually to get away from the house and the family.

Or the team returns from a losing road trip at nine or ten on a Sunday night, absolutely bushed. The jerk of a manager orders everybody to be on the field for practice at nine the next morning, killing the week's first and only day off, maddening the players and their wives, and helping no marriage one bit.

Having heard that behind every successful man stands a devoted woman, and wanting to be near their men in any case, some of the wives come to the ball games. The results can be calamitous. The Cardinals used to put all the wives in the same reserved section, but had to break them up after a couple of hair-pulling brawls.

"My husband would have won if your husband had only driven in the run," an uptight wife would shout.

Wham!

What with one thing and another, including their own disappointment about failing to make it as husbands and fathers, some players notice that eager girls are as abundant in the team's hometown as anywhere else. And as undemanding. And as consoling. And as relaxing. Not many baseball wives are oblivious to this. In some cases, Shorty turns up.

Shorty lives in the same city. He has two things going for him. First, he thinks that the player's wife is the sexiest, most charming, most neglected, most misunderstood and most lovable creature he has ever seen. Second, he has a copy of the team's road schedule. He knows exactly when it will be out of town and exactly when it will come home. One night as the player returns from the road and enters his front door, he hears the back door closing. That's Shorty, leaving Momma thirty seconds behind schedule.

My own marriage was typical of its kind and ended in total failure. I was twenty-one, Beverly was a couple of years younger, and absolutely beautiful. We mistook an immediate attraction for love. We knew little worth knowing about love, sex, responsibility, raising a family. Whatever handicaps we brought to the marriage were intensified by the tense comings and goings of the baseball season. We didn't have a chance. Not that we didn't try. Matter of fact, we tried twice, and were divorced twice. We hated to impose divorce on the children. But we had brains enough to see that an unhappy home was worse for them. Those were hard days, baby. You try to leave your domestic troubles at home and do your thing in front of 40,000 people, and your mind wanders to the bitterness and guilt. I was lucky to survive in the major leagues, considering the state I was in for a while. If I could have saved the marriage by leaving baseball, I think that I would have done so. But the problem was deeper than that.

Hence, Curt Flood, the jolly bachelor with the comfy pad on the nineteenth floor and lovely little friends the continent across. Including some extra-special ones who know me well, accept me for what I am and even understand how I got that way. I do not regard any of them as marriageable. Not by me. I'm not ready.

When my baseball career ends, I expect a long and difficult period of adjustment. I played no ball at all during 1970 but continued to think like a player. Normal hours and the other routines of everyday life remained alien to me. I preferred it that way. I needed to regard the year as a prolonged winter, an extended off-season which would be followed by a resumption of stardom. Awaiting his cherished spring, the player suspends routine. He rests, he parties, he attends to whatever negligible duties his outside businesses may require of an absentee who is but temporarily present. Mainly, he renews his tissues and refuels his mind for the next difficult baseball season—the next justification of his curious existence. And in my special case during the strange 1970, he wonders if there are to be any more seasons.

At last, it ends. The athletic celebrity recedes into a twilight. Time draws him from center stage to the wings to oblivion. It converts him from celebrity to recent celebrity to former celebrity and finally emancipates (or condemns) him to whatever he can make of himself in the world at large. Unless his emotional development was permanently arrested at an early age, he finally unwinds. He may even emerge as a reasonably whole person. He may now form human relationships on a normal, one-to-one basis, his judgments and emotions perhaps clearer than they were during his years as a social and sexual trophy.

But there is no inevitability about it. He might prefer to dwell in the past, clinging to whatever shreds of his former glamor may remain, or may be imagined or pretended. Until he sees how he turns out in that respect, he is a poor candidate for marriage. To know that much is the beginning of some kind of wisdom.

I know that much.

7

A Powerful Goodness

Whenever we played in San Francisco, my nephews and nieces would come from Oakland to cheer for me as enthusiastically as they could in rather difficult circumstances. Fate had burdened them with divided loyalties. They worshiped Willie Mays of San Francisco, yet my own claim to family encouragement could not be denied. I sometimes heard them rooting for both heroes at once, their voices as shrill as noon whistles.

"Hit that ball, Willie! Hit that ball!"

Crack!

"Catch it, Curt! Catch it!"

The San Francisco trips were reunions with them and the rest of the family, and with Jim Chambers, George Powles and Sam Bercovich, towering figures in my life. One night at the end of the 1962 season, Jim took me to visit his cousin, Marian Jorgensen, and her husband, John.

"They're great fans, Curt," he had said more than once. "They've been following your progress since the sandlot days. And they know all about your interest in painting. You'll love them."

Fans. Coming from anybody but Jim Chambers, the description would have turned me off. The typical fan is an inquisitor. Do I think that I really cover as much ground in the outfield as Mays? How come Lou Brock steals more bases than I do? Who is the best pitcher in the league? Have I ever hit a home run off him? And fans are advisors. They advise you on batting. On fielding. On managerial strategy and tactics. On trades that should be made to strengthen your team. And on and on and on. Fans foot the bills and are entitled to entertainment of the highest quality in comfortable stadiums at reasonable prices. But the curtain must come down sometimes. The athlete can't be on stage constantly. He is to be forgiven if he prefers to spend his leisure with people who think of him as a person.

I went with Jim to the dinner party because I was sure that he would not expose me to fans of the more lethal kind. But a little lethal is enough. Let us say that I accompanied Jim with misgivings.

I have relived that evening many times without being able to reduce it to everyday terms. It was a recognition— an emotional discovery bordering on the spiritual. I entered the presence of the Jorgensens and was home. Home from a long journey. Home from the wars. Home to the stability and forgiveness of home. Home where I belonged. Marian and Johnny felt the same. Jim was astounded. We did not discuss the phenomenon in explicit terms. What it boiled down to was that the Jorgensens and Flood loved each other on sight.

I was a cool customer of twenty-four, mentally quick, passably articulate, culturally and politically underdeveloped, veneered with a brittle gloss of big-league savvy. My

attitudes inclined to the gutter-tough and dugout-cynical.
An inner confidence had propelled me over many obstacles
to a highly perishable success. I had no idea where this confidence might take me next, or even whether it would remain serviceable. I had begun to realize that it derived
from a delicately balanced, ruthlessly controlled arrangement of raw nerves, the vulnerability of which was becoming more evident under the stress of a discordant marriage.
That the Jorgensens found me likable moved me, as it
should have. I needed them more than I knew. I needed
new dimensions more than I knew. On that evening, these
needs may have expressed themselves as an open-minded,
open-hearted eagerness. Marian remembers eagerness as
part of it. I never argue with her when she says nice things
about me.

John Jorgensen was thirty-five years older than I. He was
gray-haired, brown-eyed, about my height (five-nine), but
slighter. An almost jaunty step. A soft, deep voice. And a
head-on directness. It was not bluff or overbearing. Neither
was it naive. It was the directness of a man who had discovered years earlier that he could face the world without
fear and, therefore, without guile. He was as receptive as
an open doorway, and concealed as little.

Marian—Babe—was as free of affectation as her husband. She grinned exuberantly, listened intently, spoke
with uninhibited warmth, fussed over us without being fussy
about it. She reveled in her husband. I could have wept.
It was clear at once that theirs was not just an accommoda-
tion of personalities and bodies, not just the usual armed
truce. It was a marriage of total congeniality, enriched by
a deeply held philosophy of life. They were humanists.
They believed in the worth and perfectibility of man. And
in the obligations of man. And in the powers of love and
honor.

That night we discussed the politics of Oakland, of California, of the nation, of peace, of war. We discussed people, love and family. I had never experienced conversation before! Not like this. The more we talked, the more my world enlarged and the more elated I became at my incredible luck. I knew so little of life! There was so much to learn! How could these dear, generous people stand my prattle? I *knew* how! They liked me—without caring a damn whether I played center field or pushed a broom. They did not pretend that I was white. They did not pretend that they were black. They were not at all uptight. I felt as if I had been transported into the twenty-first century.

Their home was in the Montclair district of the Oakland hills. It was a fastidious place without the curse of the interior decorator on it. A place of generous comforts, warm colors, warm textures, splendid antiques. A huge living room, its ceiling vaulted and beamed. A large, well-used fireplace at one end. A library with a paradise of books from floor to ceiling. I roamed the house like an excited child that night, touching surfaces, opening books, peering through windows at views, climbing stairs, sinking into chairs. I had not more than one drink or two (afternoon game the next day), but got high on felicity. We finally embraced each other and I tore myself away.

During batting practice the next afternoon, I saw Marian come to her seat. I backed away from the plate and blew kisses to her. Excitement flurried in the batting cage. Where's the broad? Which one is it? Got something new going?

"You better believe it."

After the season ended, I brought my wife to the Jorgensens, and then they spent Thanksgiving at our place in Pomona. It occurred to me that this new friendship might confer a healing wisdom on Beverly and me. My awareness suddenly was expanding in so many directions—could it not reach inward and repair my defects as husband and father? Marian and Johnny were keen on Beverly. I asked them for advice (which they would not have given otherwise), and tried to follow it. But the Jorgensens were not miracle workers. Beverly and I limped along for several more years, apart more often than not, and finally gave up.

Johnny Jorgensen was a master craftsman, owner of an industrial engraving plant. He was an indifferent businessman, unwilling to waste energy on the techniques of management. An acknowledged genius in the painstaking art of designing and engraving industrial stamping dies, he made an ample living that way and then rushed home to Marian, where the meaning was.

He wondered if I might be interested in the work. So did I. For the second time in our relationship, I had the feeling that I had arrived home. It was as if I had been born to the craft. Like Johnny, I enjoyed the infinite detail of close work. One slip of an engraving stylus and a $12,000 die might be spoiled irreparably. Manual and visual talents were not sufficient. Neither was concern about the consequences of error. Absolute perfection was required. This was Johnny's bag. His perfectionism placed him beyond reach of error. He made a perfectionist of me. He did it by example, without once raising his voice or sharpening its tone. In time, I was taking dies every step of the way, from preliminary drawings to finished products as perfect as gems.

Johnny told me that I was the first young man he had found with the ability to succeed him in the shop. He made me his business partner. This pleased us both. It assured him the continuity of his unique craftsmanship. It assured me of a secure and pleasant place in the world after I played out my string in baseball. Not once did he suggest that a conscientious partner might quit baseball immediately to give full attention to business. Johnny did not believe that *any* business deserved full attention except in the satisfying exertions of craft.

Because money did not tempt him it could not buy him. He took the jobs he liked and rejected all others. I remember a day when he refused a contract to make a die that would have stamped "U.S. Army" on a weapon. The job was worth many thousands of dollars. "I will not profit from killing," he explained.

Anybody can spout principles, liberal or otherwise. How many men actually live by principle? Johnny was a true activist who tended his corner of the planet with immaculate honor. Anyone who disapproved of him was welcome to do so. Johnny had his own life to live. It took courage. I gathered that many of the Jorgensens' acquaintances and most of their friends had long since written them off as oddballs or pinks or, by whatever label, disturbers. The era of mindlessness had begun. Patriotism was being mistaken for subservience to authority. Honor was being attended to by pasting emblems on the windows or bumpers of automobiles. Persons of substance were supposed to behave predictably and not voice so many upstream ideas about peace, integration and the dignity of man.

Johnny and Marian and I were closer than friends, freer and easier than family. He and I would tear back to the house after work, soak up a few martinis, consume one of Babe's good dinners, and sit for hours at the table, strumming ukeleles, singing songs and inevitably resuming the endlessly stimulating conversational brawl that had begun on my first visit. My mother and father and sisters and brothers often joined us there and so did numerous ball players. The place was a sanctuary of warm fellowship, a joy and comfort beyond description.

Marian converted the downstairs play area into an apartment for me. Home now became home in fact as well as in feeling. The Jorgensens were entirely unimpressed to learn that the constant black traffic was not a hit with the community. Darkies in the neighborhood at night were just about the last straw for locals already baffled by the relaxed and nonconforming Jorgensens. When I raised the question, Marian dazzled me with a typical Marianism, "Good Heavens, dear! They don't understand *us*, but we understand *them!* We wouldn't dream of telling them how to run their lives, so we surely can't let them run ours."

After the Cardinals won the 1964 World Series, my wife and I made another run at marriage. We found a delightful house and pool in a place called Alamo, near Mount Diablo in Alameda County, about twenty minutes from Oakland. We had scarcely signed the papers when the agent tried to get us to change our minds.

"I have a home you might like better."

"We want the one we've taken."

"Won't you at least look at this one?"

"No."

I needed no diagram. Somebody in the new neighborhood had found out who—or what—was moving in. Matter of fact, the boyfriend of the former owner had announced that he would lay down his glorious life before any nigger would occupy the house in which he, *he* had slept. We were told that he had posted himself in the driveway with a shotgun.

During the hectic days of negotiation that followed, Marian converted her own place into a command post and message center for us and the lawyers and cops and other interested parties. During the height of the excitement, somebody cut her telephone wires in what I took to be a gesture of neighborhood solidarity. That is, the solidarity between her neighbors and the poor souls miles away on whom I was inflicting myself and my family.

On the appointed day, Marian and Beverly, the police and a lawyer and I arrived at the Alamo house with fists full of writs and injunctions. The armed defender of white supremacy was nowhere in sight. He was rumored to be sitting in a van with shotgun cocked. He also was rumored to be barricaded in the house, ready for action. After we broke down the door (he had changed all the locks), we found the place empty. If he had been there, I might have had to fight Marian. I could sense that she was preparing to fling herself at the gun, to prevent injury to anyone else.

And so, on this beautiful late fall day, with the sun brightly shining and the hills rolling green all around, the Floods moved into their new home. Some neighbors took us out to dinner and made us feel welcome. A few days later, the lady next door came around to thank us for moving in. It was nice, she said, to have decent people in the place. The previous occupants had been noisy, she said, and had done a lot of boozily conspicuous skinny-dipping in the pool.

One afternoon I found my little girl weeping. Her new playmates all belonged to a Brownie troop. She had asked to join and had been turned down. Because only whiteys were Brownies. I briefly considered appealing to the adult leaders of the organization. "Can't you grant us an exemption?" I would plead. "We are *respectable!* We don't even skinny-dip in the pool." And for a longer moment, I considered strangling somebody to avenge the sadness of a little brown girl.

Everything went to pieces after that. We finally moved the hell out of there, our domesticity taxed beyond the breaking point once more. Through it all, the Jorgensens were patient and generous. They had become part of my identity, and I of theirs. Apart from my performance as husband and father in a situation beyond retrieve, I was becoming a sounder and more substantial person, I think, and a more discerning and effective one.

The Jorgensens' wide interests aroused an intellectual hunger in me. I rushed to books and gorged myself. I could feel myself growing and changing. Johnny and Marian's daily example taught me to place a higher value on life than I had in the past. Cherishing life as they did, they refused to degrade it in others or suppress it in themselves. I strove to emulate this, wanting now to serve my own principles as best I could, rather than float through the years like a leaf in the wind. Whatever I contributed to the unique morale of the Cardinals was part of this growth, and so, of course, was my decision to have it out in public with the owners of organized baseball.

Late in 1966, I was visiting a friend in Hollywood when word came by telephone that Johnny Jorgensen had been murdered. His body had been found in the plant, hacked to pieces. I got the next plane, arrived at the house blind with grief, and found Marian in collapse. The police took me downtown.

They explained that it was customary to begin these investigations by questioning the immediate family and any business associates or others who might conceivably benefit from death. I was Mr. Jorgensen's partner, right? Okay, step this way.

I was absolutely out of my tree, with no idea of what had happened or why, frantic with worry about Marian, and perishing inside with my own loss. They gave me the bare-walled-room-and-unshaded-light-bulb routine. They strapped me into a lie detector. They asked me where I had been the night before. I told them "Los Angeles," and the needle jumped because I had been in Hollywood. If I had not known that I had an alibi, the atmosphere of interrogation would have made me feel guilty. As it was, I did feel guilty. It should have been I, not Johnny. It should have been anyone but Johnny and Marian.

They even gave Marian the lie detector test. The poor thing did not want to live. She had died with her husband. A life full of meaning had ended meaninglessly, as if meaning were a delusion and life a fraud. I clung to her because I loved her and grieved for her and because she and I could not give up now without denying the meaning of Johnny, who had personified the usefulness and purposefulness of life.

We eventually pulled through, although I never mustered the courage to go near the engraving shop again, and cannot bear to enter any engraving shop, anywhere. After bugging our phones and following us around for two weeks, the police finally caught the murderer. He was a black adolescent who had gone on a psychotic rampage after being dismissed from a job. He had never seen Johnny until the moment he stumbled into the plant and lashed out in mindless fury. They sent him to an institution for the criminally insane.

I tried to persuade Babe to move to St. Louis with me, but she would not budge. She needed to get herself together by herself. Moreover, she suffers from a weakness that may be rather widespread among the good: she gives indefatigably and without stint, but she hesitates to take. "I shouldn't be a burden to you, dear," was her theme. I telephoned her frequently throughout the 1967 season, but made no headway.

On the Cardinals' last trip to San Francisco that year, I phoned and demanded that she meet me for lunch at

Diamond Jim's, a favorite haunt of ours in Oakland. I poured a couple of Bloody Marys into her.

"Now, look," I said, "you have to come to St. Louis and live with me."

"No."

"Now, damnit, Babe, listen here. At least come back to St. Louis and see a couple of the World Series games. I need you, Babe. I really need you. Come back there and you'll see how much."

I had finally hit on the correct approach. I *needed* her, therefore the proposal began to make some sense to the dear old chick. I could have kicked myself. My need was real and my words were true, and I had not been sensitive enough to put the question in that way before.

She agreed to come to the Series. My mother came with her. They had a grand time. And Marian realized that I was lost without her. My apartment was a shambles. My finances were a shame. My personal life was scandalous. And furthermore, she was my dearest, closest friend. We were in each other's blood. She said that she would move East in a few months.

On the night before her departure from California, she visited her son, Fritz, and then set out to drive home for the last time. On the winding road above San Pablo Dam, a deer darted in front of the car. She tried to avoid it, but could not. The impact sent her car hurtling down the canyon toward the reservoir, three or four hundred feet below. About halfway to the bottom, the car struck a tree and stopped. Marian may have been dazed for a while. She recalls saying to herself, "This has to be ridiculous. I'm supposed to be leaving for St. Louis tomorrow." She was uninjured, except for some leg cuts. And she discovered that she could get out of the car. She did so and dragged her bad self through the dark all the way up the heavily thicketed hill. She even found her purse on the way. When she got to the road, a motorist saw her and took her to the police. He was a black brother, a nice touch in the circumstances.

The police said that if the car's lights had broken, the gasoline might have exploded and that would have been that. But the lights remained intact and bright, which was the only reason that they were able to find the car later that night in the dense brush.

She came to St. Louis and took command. She runs my house. She is my secretary and partner. She keeps track of my portrait commissions. She spoils me rotten.

People's curiosity sometimes overcomes them. "You still living with that white woman?" they asked. Or a chick will hesitate about coming up for a drink: "That white lady still there?" I seldom give a detailed answer, which would be that the lady is my partner and my friend and that I love and honor her. Marian's dignity needs no defense.

8

Carl of My Blood

My brother Carl's incessant skirmishes with schools, shopkeepers, neighbors and police tended to distract parental attention from the rest of us. It seemed to me that my well-scrubbed industriousness was worthy of notice in its own right. I resented this but idolized Carl. He was one of the best young athletes in Oakland, a city full of outstanding athletes. He also could paint, write, talk up a storm and bowl over girls with a glance. I had no desire to join him in his troubles, but the stirrings of my own adolescence made me want to share his fun. I often asked him to take me along on his nightly adventures.

"Stay home, you little devil," he would say. "You're not going my way. Just stick to business, hear?"

He did not discuss his affairs with me. It was taken for granted between us that his life was a ghetto scenario of desperate danger and small hope, and that his options were expiring. The next-to-last bus had left Disasterville. He did not know if he would get himself together and grasp a final opportunity to escape. He was not sure that the opportunity would even present itself. I speak of him now as he was at seventeen, when I was fifteen.

My name had begun to appear in the local sport pages. He was proud of that, and vigilant against any influence (especially his own) that might have deflected me from my course. I had no clear conception of what that course might be, but he did. It was as if he had appointed me his representative in the world. I was going to scratch and scramble my way out of that ghetto if it was the last thing Carl ever accomplished. I now realize that we could have come out together, if he had not been differently bent. He had every bit as much athletic talent as I, perhaps more, and was considerably bigger and stronger. I have no doubt whatever that he would have been a major-league star. But he lost interest in baseball before he finished the eleventh grade.

A few years ago, he won a national chess championship. His restless, disturbing abstract paintings have won awards. He reads four languages. During a few weeks in my employ, he proved himself a brilliant salesman. He is a voracious reader with discriminating tastes and a remarkable gift of scholarship. For example, the chess and languages were self-taught.

Every Thursday afternoon, Marian Jorgensen drives to Jefferson City, Missouri, and puts up at a motel. The next morning she goes to the state penitentiary to visit Carl, who is serving twenty years for armed robbery. Between visits, he writes her at least one letter a day. She answers them all. She should be more sparing of herself. But if she were, she would not be Marian. And if she were not Marian, we'd all be in a hell of a fix.

When I first met the Jorgensens, Carl was doing a Federal stretch in Leavenworth. At our second or third meeting, it seemed to me that Johnny and Babe were entitled to know about this, so I told them. They already knew. A relative in the Oakland police had volunteered the information when he learned that the Jorgensens had befriended me. Marian and Carl began corresponding with each other, and she soon was immersed in his problems.

Carl's stay in Leavenworth was his first experience in a penitentiary. He and some of his nocturnal companions had decided to enter the bank robbery business and had pulled three successful jobs, stashing the proceeds in an abandoned tenement. One of the group was caught and promptly disclosed where the money was hidden. The Federal Bureau of Investigation then posted agents at the tenement and hauled in the rest of the gang one by one, as each arrived to replenish his bankroll.

If Carl's were not a first-rate intelligence, the episode would have been merely distressing and somewhat ludicrous. What made it ghastly was the spirit of hopeless, inevitable defeat that accounted for the almost deliberate suppression of intelligence. Carl was too bright to continue robbing banks until his arrest became a matter of top priority with the FBI. Yet he did it. And he was much too bright to go to the hiding place after some of his partners had been picked up. Yet he did that, too. So instead of pitching in the World Series or painting in Paris, he solicited punishment in Leavenworth. It was there that he learned a few languages and became, by mail, the champion chess player among his country's prisoners.

Having satisfied herself that Carl was a person of extreme sensitivity and by no means a stereotype of the hardened jailbird, Marian swung into action. Her major premise was that he had been in the penitentiary long enough. She was convinced that prolonged confinement would lead to an emotional deterioration which would ruin Carl without helping society. In other words, she was challenging the entire philosophy of the American penal system. After she had expended four strenuous years and much of her modest resources, Carl was free.

She began by chatting with the FBI man who had arrested my brother. Whatever his opinion of Carl may have been, he acknowledged that Marian had every legal right to intercede, feeling as she did about the case. She then began commuting to the Federal Bureau of Prisons in Washington, D.C. She consulted lawyers. She conferred with the trial judge. She queried. She hounded. She cited precedent. She finally got Carl transferred from Leavenworth to McNeil Island Penitentiary in the State of Washington, to be nearer. Meanwhile, she and Johnny took care of his wife and four children.

One day at McNeil, Carl turned a corner and found two prisoners beating a guard. One was chopping the man with the business end of a hoe. The other was kicking him. Carl tore them away, noticed that the guard was turning blue, surmised that he had swallowed his tongue, freed it, and saved the man's life. He would have done exactly the same thing if two guards had been brutalizing a prisoner. But no prisoner knew this and few would have cared. Penitentiary inmates are frugal with their compassion. To many, the rescue of a guard is an act of treachery. Carl was branded a fink, a friend of the establishment, fit only for extermination.

They inserted double-edged razor blades in his cake of soap: Showering, he cut his chest to shreds before feeling pain or noticing blood. They smeared excrement on his bed. They destroyed his paintings. Someone fired a ball bearing at him, probably with a slingshot. The missile embedded itself in his skull and had to be removed surgically.

Marian and I visited the trial judge. She described events

at McNeil. "There simply is no point in keeping him incarcerated, Your Honor," she concluded. "Not with his life in danger." She said it without tears or stridence, without wheedling or whining. She said it quietly, yet with ringing force. Call it the force of humanity. She towered above us all. I felt like leaping up and giving her an ovation.

The judge apparently agreed that the hideous situation justified extraordinary measures. He declared Carl eligible for immediate parole. The parole board denied the application. Shortly thereafter the Supreme Court of the United States handed down its famous decision of June 1966 (*Miranda* v. *State of Arizona*), which nullified the criminal convictions of persons who had been denied legal advice or the right of silence. On these grounds, Carl was resentenced and placed on probation. He walked away from McNeil Island in one piece.

"There's nothing that ever will put me behind bars again," he told me. "Nothing. No way."

Johnny Jorgensen put him to work in the engraving shop. But then, all of a sudden, there was no engraving shop. When I moved back to St. Louis in 1967, I hoped to find something there for Carl, to get him as far from the Oakland ghetto as possible.

I became involved in a scheme designed to make a real-estate investor of the common man. Known as an investment trust, the plan resembled a mutual fund, except that it dealt in real estate rather than stocks. Carl was just the man to handle sales in the black community. While waiting for the enterprise to jell (it never did), I could keep my brother busy helping me in my portrait business, which had begun to expand.

My sketches of other baseball players had appeared in newspapers from time to time without electrifying the world of art. The situation began to change after I did a photographically precise oil portrait of the Cardinals' owner, August A. Busch, Jr. He was so delighted with it that he hung it in the saloon of his yacht. Other commissions began to come in. My portrait of Martin Luther King was reproduced in the tens of thousands. I appeared with some of my work on the network television show, "Today." Dozens of inquiries arrived in the mail. I was in business.

I brought Carl to St. Louis and told him to sit around my apartment as long as he pleased, until he felt comfortably acclimated. I paid him $100 per week. If he felt like trying to sell Curt Flood oil portraits, he could keep half of the proceeds. He felt like it. He was a fantastic salesman. He could walk into a restaurant with that big-eyed, sensitive, enthusiastic face of his, charm everyone immediately, whip out a sample of Curt Flood's work, and walk away with two or three orders at a time. When he was in form, he made me wish that I had four hands and a fifty-six-hour day. To keep up with the demand, I abandoned the sittings of conventional portraiture and worked from snapshots or other photographs. I even mechanized the preliminary phases of the work, saving time. The finished products were photographically representational. The really good ones were more than photographic.

I noticed that Carl's efforts were rather uneven. I did not know that he was into narcotics. I would come home at night, find him trembling in a cold sweat, and believe his story about having a touch of the flu. As usual, Marian bore the brunt. She conspired with him to protect me from the truth. He hated to multiply his remorse by sharing it with his allegedly clean-cut little brother. He wanted to kick the habit. By himself. Cold turkey.

I have no idea when it all started. He may have been on some kind of junk when he got into that bank robbery mess on the Coast—so many of the ghetto cats were. Marian and he contend that his battle with the hard stuff began in Oakland when he came down with severe chest pains, went to a ghetto physician and was given a bottle of morphine tablets. Lord knows what caused the chest pains. They might have been muscular, or an attack of heartburn. In any event, Carl became physically dependent on the morphine and finally went over the brink.

Oblivious as ever, I trotted off to spring training in March 1969, and Carl retired to his room to sweat himself out of his habit. Guess who stayed at his side from Friday afternoon until Monday morning while he pleaded with his demons, cursed his pain, tore his flesh and quite literally tried to climb the walls. Marian suffered as he suffered. In his agony, he could have overpowered her, left the apartment and found a fix. Instead, he seemed to draw strength from her. He endured his torment. When Monday dawned, he appeared to be coming out of the ordeal in fairly good shape.

Whereupon the almighty dollar defeated us. We were just getting started with Curt Flood & Associates, Inc., the prime activity of which was a commercial photography business. The enterprise looked promising from where I sat, celebrity-fashion, on its outer fringes, but it was doomed. Marian could not foresee that in March 1969. Nobody could. Marian had urgent appointments to keep—the details of equipment purchases, or something. She asked Carl if he could go to sleep for a while. He said that he was feeling much better and would surely sleep. He promised not to leave the apartment. He would rest and await her return. Much heartened, she left for her business engagements. Not long afterward, he also left.

The morning ended for Carl in a downtown alley, after he and an acquaintance thoroughly botched an attempt to hold up a jewelry store. One of the stars of the incident was a television cameraman who happened to be present when the getaway car (property of the St. Louis Police Department) crashed into a pole. No reason why it should not have. A policeman had just shot holes in its rear tires. With the TV tape grinding away, the policeman walked to the window on the driver's side and put a pistol to Carl's head.

"Go ahead and shoot," said my brother.

Marian understood and forgave him. In self-defense I turned him off, shut him out, pronounced him nonexistent. Enough was enough. I could not sustain that attitude, of course. A year after his imprisonment, I was telling a friend how prideful and protective of me Carl had been as a youngster, and how he had tried (albeit ineffectively) to shelter me from unpleasantness ever after.

This pleased Marian. "It's so wonderful to hear Curt speak that way of Carl," she beamed. "The bitterness is being worked out of his heart. It isn't good to carry that kind of feeling, you know."

She then withdrew to her room. She had to write him a letter. Then she had to renew his subscription to the *Chess Review*.

9

Whim as a Way of Life

Just as Honus Wagner will always be remembered as a great shortstop, he will never be forgotten for his arithmetic. Early in the century, when he was the star of the Pittsburgh Pirates, he rejected a $2,000 contract offered by the club owner, Barney Dreyfus.

"Not on your life," bellowed the shrewd Honus. "I won't play for a penny less than *fifteen hundred* dollars."

In later years, Dreyfus told the story with enormous relish (but not in Wagner's presence). He recalled that he had been unable to withstand the player's argument and had succumbed to the demand without protest. Anyone who wonders why the Pittsburgh team is called the Pirates might consider the business practices of its founder.

The players of my generation are more worldly. A few cannot read their own press clippings or write a letter home, but they all know the difference between fifteen hundred and two thousand. The ability to make such fine distinctions proves that we moderns are not entirely helpless in

our salary negotiations with management. Helpless, yes,
Entirely, no.

Eavesdrop on a private conversation among typical ball
players at contract-signing time.

"Who the hell *built* that goddamned stadium for them?"

"Yeah."

"I'll tell you who. *We* did. Those people come to see *us*.
Dig?"

"The bastards try to cut me ten percent because my
average fell off twenty points. But when it went up forty
points the year before, I had all I could do to get a fifteen
percent raise."

"The sons-of-bitches are giving that rookie a lot of publicity to pressure me into signing. They can go shove it."

"Are you going to hold out?"

"Brother, I'd love to. But I can't afford it."

"They've got us by the seeds."

"You better believe it."

And more of the same.

Required to negotiate his contract in individual, eye-to-
eye discussion with the general manager, without the helpful presence of a lawyer or a talent representative, the
ordinary player is outgunned. His inexperience as a bar-
gainer is only one of his disadvantages. The know-how of
the general manager is another. But the fundamental
handicap is baseball's reserve system, the iron provisions of
which make individual negotiation a mockery. The player
who refuses to sign on the employer's terms remains bound
to the club. He can be forced to work at reduced wages
without signing, unless he chooses to abandon his career
altogether. No other team can hire him until his official
owner clears the way by selling or trading his contract,
which then becomes the exclusive property of the new
owner.

An inevitable consequence of this system is that baseball players perform for lower salaries than they could negotiate for themselves in an open market. Whether viewed individually or as a group, baseball players do not get their fair share of the industry's receipts.

What do I mean by "fair"? To develop some basis for judgment, let us consider wage and salary levels in other industries. Government studies show that in manufacturing, where the purchase of raw materials is a considerable item, production workers get a relatively low percentage of the employer's gross revenue. On the average, their wages account for about 24 percent of receipts. The percentage varies from industry to industry, of course, and from corporation to corporation. For example, U.S. Steel reports that it pays its own workers 40 percent.

The percentage tends to become much higher in industries that supply services rather than manufactured goods. In various segments of the entertainment business, the performing talent is rewarded with more than 50 percent of the receipts.

But not in that branch of entertainment known as major-league ball. Baseball's own unaudited estimates show that the players get 20 percent of the industry's total income. Quite properly included in this percentage is the almost $5.5 million paid annually by the owners into the players' Benefit Plan, which is known loosely as a "pension plan" but really is a system of deferred salary payments plus health insurance. One may assume that the official statistic also includes wages paid to minor-league performers during September, when they join the parent teams for a few weeks of big-time competition.

At any rate, 20 percent is a paltry slice of the gross. In 1929, when baseball salaries were much lower, the percentage was 35. The players' share has been declining ever

since, especially in recent years, when baseball's revenues
from television have been rising dramatically. According
to the club owners' latest economic study, which was
presented in evidence at the trial of my suit before Judge
Irving Ben Cooper in the U.S. District Court for the Southern District of New York, the average salary of a major-
league baseball player was above $28,000 during 1970. The
Major League Baseball Players Association presents the
matter in clearer perspective. During 1969, says the Association, most major-league players made $20,000 or less.
Indeed, 18 percent of the players got $10,000—the mini-
mum then permissible under the contract between the
owners and the Association. A small number of large salaries make the average misleadingly high.

In 1969, the player payroll of major-league baseball was
about $20 million. Baseball's revenue from television was
$50 million. This meant that the owners were $30 million
in the black (as far as the cost of performing talent was
concerned) before the first fan of 1969 parked his car,
bought his ticket, obtained his souvenir program and began
consuming overpriced hot dogs and beer. The Association
estimates baseball's revenues from all sources at $150
million per year—not counting spin-off benefits such as Mr.
Busch's sales of Mr. Busch's beer to the concessionaire in
the baseball park named after Mr. Busch. And the promo-
tion of Mr. Wrigley's chewing gum. And the benefits that
might be harvested when a Columbia Broadcasting System
purchases the New York Yankees.

One substantial factor in the operating expenses of a
major-league baseball team is the cost of player development. The clubs spend millions to maintain large scouting
staffs and networks of minor-league farm clubs (which
usually make no money). To this must be added the

bonuses and salaries paid to young players during their years as minor leaguers.

This system is quite irrational. The owners could save millions by abandoning the wastefulness of competitive scouting. If the activity were staffed and administered by the league (or jointly by both leagues) instead of by the individual club, the cost of scouting could be greatly reduced. Nobody need fear that such centralization would destroy the competitiveness of the sport. Except on the field of play, the industry is blandly noncompetitive. Like the international cartelists whom they resemble so closely in all respects, the owners divide their market to suit each other's financial convenience—assigning new franchises and permitting the transfer of old ones. Similarly, they share cooperatively in the "raw materials" of the industry, by means of a free-agent draft that assigns each promising high-school or college player to one prospective employer and no other. No, a cooperative scouting system would reduce gross expenditures without affecting the spirit of the game one little bit.

Why, then, the perpetuation of a less efficient approach to player procurement and development? Setting aside stand-pattism, which is as pronounced in this industry as in any other, one may conclude that these activities are not quite as costly as the owners maintain. Perhaps the clubs spend as much as they say. Perhaps. But they get a good deal of it back. For example, money spent on the upkeep of farm teams is not without some return. Even an unprofitable minor-league team sells some tickets. And the player who finally gets to the major leagues after receiving perhaps $30,000 in minor-league salaries, plus a bonus, does not represent a loss of $30,000. He becomes a bookkeeping entry of considerable importance at tax time.

As if he were the team bus or any other chattel subject to fair wear-and-tear, the ball club is permitted to depreciate him on its tax returns. The more he cost and the greater his presumed value, the more is written off.

It now can be seen that the investment in development is repaid to some extent. Moreover, as Mr. Justice Arthur Goldberg pointed out for me in a post-trial brief, "The cost of player development is largely a numbers game. Major-league players represent the cream of their profession. If General Motors assigned all junior executive salaries as the cost of producing senior executives, 'executive development costs' would be enormous."

Which reminds me that the baseball industry reports an increase in "general administrative" expenses. Those costs include salaries and other disbursements to club executives, including individuals involved in actual team ownership. In 1969, more than 19 percent of baseball's total revenue was expended in this way, the figures showed. In short, the industry professes to spend as much on administrators as on talent. Either the talent is underpaid or the front office is overpaid. Be that as it may, administrative expenses would be reduced substantially if the competitive scouting system were centralized.

As I interpret baseball's recital of its financial woes, the situation is peachy for the fans and players, but the owners bear a heavy load. All that stands between the Good of the Game and utter havoc is the arrangement that exempts the owners from the hardships imposed on all other interstate entrepreneurs by the nation's antitrust laws. Should a court order, a Congressional statute or a players' strike weaken the owners' control of their livestock, the game might perish.

According to this pessimistic theory, if baseball players were as free to shop for employment as actors are, the

richest club would hire all the stars, making a shambles of
every pennant race. The implication is that some teams are
too poor to compete for talent in an open market. The
present reserve system protects them from that catastrophe.
Reduced to its essentials, the argument suggests that baseball players now subsidize their employers by working at
cut rates. And that the courts, Congress and the public
should perpetuate this unique state of affairs. For the Good
of the Game.

The whole spiel is sheer humbug, of course. No major-
league baseball corporation is presently in financial straits.
If any were, it seems to me that subsidies should come not
from the employees but from the suffering owner's fellow
monopolists. Let them pass the hat. Or, if baseball be
essential to the national morale, as its proprietors claim,
the government itself might support the owners with grants
or tax abatements, just as it supports railroads, airlines and
oil wells. Unless I misread history, we have passed the
stage when indentured servitude was justifiable on grounds
that the employer could not afford the cost of normal labor.

Which reminds me that the word *slavery* has arisen in
connection with my lawsuit. I have been needled for using
the word. Who ever heard of a $90,000-per-year slave? The
idea is considered farcical. I concede that the condition of
the major-league baseball player is closer to peonage than
to slavery. Yet I am content to stand with sentiments expressed in 1949 by Judge Jerome N. Frank of the U.S.
Circuit Court of Appeals in the case of Danny Gardella,
a player who had been victimized by the reserve system:

"If the players be regarded as quasi-peons, it is of no
moment that they are well paid. Only the totalitarian-
minded will believe that high pay excuses virtual slavery."

Resuming our discussion of the ruin toward which I am
supposedly propelling baseball, I should like to point out

that ruin comes in more forms than one. When baseball's spokesmen use the term, they refer not to insolvency but to reduced profits.

Baseball is as secretive about its profit-and-loss statements as accountancy permits, but certain facts can be cited to demonstrate that the industry is in splendid condition.

Item: The Seattle Pilots were publicized as a financial disaster during 1969, the team's one year of existence. The owners had paid $5.25 million for the franchise. During this supposedly disappointing season, the paid attendance in Seattle was larger than the paid attendance of the Chicago White Sox, Cleveland Indians, Philadelphia Phillies or San Diego Padres. The average businessman might have regarded this as a promising start. He also might have been prepared to lose money for several years, while endearing himself and his ball team to the local fans. Instead, the franchise was sold and transferred to Milwaukee. The price was $10.8 million—twice what the Seattle group had paid a year earlier. One may presume that the owners would have sold out for considerably less if they had been hurting as desperately as claimed.

Item: Not long ago, Cincinnati was regarded as the worst franchise in organized ball. Bill DeWitt bought it for $2 million. Four years later, he sold it for $6 million.

Item: Employers have every right to cry poor mouth when manipulating the press and public. But the labor laws of the United States require them to behave when engaging in collective bargaining with their hired hands. A corporation that professes financial inability to meet an economic demand is obliged to substantiate the claim by showing its books. No baseball club does this. When they reject proposals made by the Major League Baseball Players Association, the club owners offer ritual instead of reason. "We are not claiming inability to pay. We simply do not consider your idea appropriate. We believe that the present meal allowances are more than satisfactory."

Perhaps it now can be agreed that bankruptcy does not loom. And that financial hardships suffered by individual clubs could be relieved by drawing on profits amassed by other branches of the combine.

The notion that one or two clubs would gobble up all the star players is contrary to the established fact that the proprietors of baseball want only to get along with each other. General Motors would employ all the best automotive designers and engineers if it could. DuPont would monopolize all the best paint and plastics salesmen. International Business Machines would corner the best electronic scientists. The very nature of free enterprise prevents this. And the sweetheart relationship between baseball's proprietors is an American staple, and would not disappear with the reserve clause.

Like other human beings, baseball players crave stability and continuity. They want to live, work and grow old in familiar, congenial surroundings. Having found a niche in life, they are unlikely to dislodge themselves, terminate various business and social relationships and move to strange communities for no reason other than an extra few thousand dollars a year.

Younger players, hungry for opportunities, might want to keep moving until they find the teams whose needs match their own. Established players might want to move after disagreements with management. But turnover would not be rapid if players were freer to choose employers than they are now. Indeed, turnover could scarcely be more rapid than it is. Fewer than half the players on 1965 rosters were with the same teams in 1970. Of the twenty player representatives who signed the industry's basic agreement in

1968, more than half were no longer with the same teams in 1970.

Enough. The entire debate about the possible consequences of abolishing the reserve clause is academic. Worse than that, it is synthetic. No adversary of baseball's obsolete employment practices has ever suggested that each player be free to negotiate with all major-league clubs before deciding where to spend the ensuing season. Granted, the Major League Baseball Players Association and I have contended that the reserve system is unconstitutional and should be outlawed. Concurrently, however, and for many years, the Association has proposed numerous alternative systems, any of which would protect the industry from the chaos it fears, yet would grant the players a degree of freedom now denied them.

As of August 1970, and for some years before, the barons of major-league baseball had refused to negotiate any of these proposals. Their press agents depicted us as total abolitionists, merchants of destruction. When not foretelling the ruination of "poor" clubs and the runaway victories of star-laden "rich" clubs as disasters to the Good of the Game, the owners spoke darkly of "tampering."

Let me offer a sample of this particular fantasy. John Doe is the star of his team, batting .400 and collecting an annual salary of $125,000. At the height of the pennant race, after he arrives in Mudville for the crucial series, a man visits his hotel room.

"Doe," says the visitor, "if you strike out with men on base during the forthcoming crucial series on which the whole shebang depends, thereby lousing up the Integrity of the Game and bilking the entire citizenry of the U.S.A., we are prepared to offer you $175,000 to play for us next year."

The man represents the Mudville team! He is bribing

Doe to throw the series! Doe flings himself to his knees and licks the man's hand, eager to get a $50,000 raise in pay!

Preposterous? The owners evidently do not think so. They have been peddling this script for years. They do not credit their own integrity. They believe themselves capable of bribery. And they are convinced that players would be susceptible to it.

I call this a delusion, and for good reasons. In the first place, the player bribed in that way would scarcely inspire confidence in the people who bribed him. Who wants to employ a sell-out artist? In the second place, if any bribing is to be done, the present system would be ideal for it. Assuming that players are amenable to overtures of this kind, which I doubt, the present system permits direct cash bribery without improved contracts or other embellishments.

Furthermore, I resent the use of the word *tampering*. One may attempt to influence the play of a professional athlete, but one does not "tamper" with him. One tampers with figures or a cash register, not with a human being. As usual, baseball's terminology betrays its essential attitudes, which are those of animal husbandry. Baseball regards us as sheep, livestock with which higher forms of life may tamper at will. No wonder we are conditioned to talk the way we do. In the pregame interview and the postgame wrap-up, and finally in his nightmares, the player dutifully recites, "Baseball has been good to me. I love the game. Baseball has been good to me. . . ."

And he has been good to baseball. He has played his heart out. He wants the industry to prosper. He wants to share in that prosperity now, and he probably hopes to make a place for himself in the game later on, being prepared for a life in baseball and little else. Through the

Major League Baseball Players Association, he and his professional colleagues (with little dissent), have attempted to negotiate an improvement in the reserve system. Not abolition. Improvement. They have submitted the following ideas for consideration by the owners:

1. The owner's option on a player's services should no longer be perpetual. It should terminate after a period of years, the length of which could be standardized by negotiation between the owners and the Association.

2. The owner's option might terminate if the player's salary had not risen in accordance with a schedule of increases that could be standardized by negotiation.

3. The motion picture industry's system of long-term contracts might be considered, including the provision that allows the performer to reopen salary negotiations at fixed intervals.

4. A player who wants to move to another club might be given the right to "play out his option," under procedures similar to those of professional football and basketball.

5. The club might have the right to retain the services of a player whose option had expired, simply by matching the salary offered by a rival club.

6. A limitation could be placed on the number of free agents that any single club could employ. This would prevent monopolization of talent by wealthier corporations.

7. Salary disagreements between a club and a player could be submitted to impartial arbitration.

At this writing no negotiation of these proposals has been undertaken by the laggards of baseball. The year might as well be 1881, and James Abram Garfield the president of the United States.

10

Discord Backstage

In 1946, our national pastime suffered grave embarrassment. A Mexican league committed the nuisance of offering professional salaries to baseball players. Defying threats of lifetime exclusion from the mainstream of the sport, some excellent performers migrated. It was understandable. Many of them had been bringing home paychecks no larger than those of semiskilled factory hands.

The Mexican skirmish was one of two interrelated crises confronted by baseball during that year. In tardy acknowledgment of a technique used by highly paid employees in other branches of the entertainment business, some baseball players finally formed a union. A union!

Its organizer was Robert Murphy, a Harvard-educated lawyer who had been an examiner for the National Labor Relations Board. During the spring training season of this momentous year, he announced the establishment of the American Baseball Guild, registered it as a labor organization and began touring the major-league camps at his own expense.

Murphy's program was modest. He felt that the major leagues should adopt a pension plan. He thought that salaries should not fall below a negotiated minimum. He believed that the club should defray the players' expenses during spring training. He advocated procedures for the resolution of players' grievances.

When spring training ended, the American Baseball Guild had organized majority support on six of the sixteen teams which then composed the major leagues. The Guild's greatest strength was on the Pittsburgh Pirates, 90 percent of whose players had joined. Murphy decided to concentrate his efforts there. In May, he demanded that the Pirate management recognize the union as collective-bargaining representative for the players. Not unpredictably, the management declined.

On June 6, a majority of the players voted to strike on the following night unless the club agreed to an immediate representation election. If favorable to the union, such an election would have bound the front office to negotiate. The management refused. On the next night, the players decided to take another strike vote. This time, they agreed that the issue was so grave that no strike should be held unless two-thirds of them supported it. A majority voted for the strike. But the majority fell short of the required two-thirds. There was no strike. From that day forward, the Pirate front office refused absolutely to discuss recognition of the American Baseball Guild.

In those days, the Commissioner of Baseball was Happy Chandler, an occasional Kentucky governor and U.S. senator, who had succeeded the imposing Judge Kenesaw Mountain Landis as the owners' chief steward of the Good of the Game. In 1951, the by-then-deposed Chandler reminisced for a Congressional committee about the hectic situation in Pittsburgh five years earlier. The celebrated pitcher Rip Sewell, an infielder named Jimmy Brown and an unnamed employee of his own office had acted as his agents, Chandler said. In his words, "They beat the union." That is, they tattled on it, and kept the other players in a state of confusion.

In August 1946, the Pennsylvania Labor Relations Board held a representation election among the Pirates. The players rejected Murphy's Guild by a vote of 15 to 3. Murphy never was heard from again. But the day may come when players will enshrine him in their own Hall of Fame. As soon as the Guild was defeated, the major leagues established a pension plan and announced that the minimum salary henceforth would be $5,000. Furthermore, they inaugurated an unprecedented policy of paying each player $25 a week for spring training expenses. To this day, the spring stipend is known as "Murphy Money." And finally, in lieu of unionization, the owners advised the players to elect their own representatives—one from each team—to confer periodically with owners about matters of mutual concern. As if to emphasize that baseball was one big happy family, the owners of most teams relieved the players of indecision about which of them might be the likeliest choice as representative. These managements chose the player representatives themselves, a practice that endured on some clubs for many years.

During those early years, the routine responsibilities of what came to be known as the Major League Baseball Players Association were less demanding than those of a legitimate labor organization. Every winter the player representatives were invited to a special meeting with the club owners. Each representative occupied a chair adjacent to that of his boss. A spokesman would then read a consolidated list of "requests." Not demands. Not proposals. Requests. The meeting then adjourned. Later, the owners would convene without the players. During the following spring, they would announce their decisions. The usual practice was to grant three or four of the pleas, deny others and ignore most.

The records of those negotiations reveal that the decision to grant a request did not necessarily mean it would be acted upon. Most of the grievances were along the lines of inoperative clubhouse plumbing, splintered dugout benches and the number of free tickets to which players were entitled. These issues were trivial in comparison with the fundamental inequities of baseball life, of course. But the Association was not supposed to deal with fundamentals. The Association was not supposed to alarm or annoy the owners. The owners ran the Association. It was a company union.

Trouble finally arose when the Commissioner of Baseball violated tradition by abandoning his role as the owners' enforcer. For one mad moment, Chandler behaved, Heaven help us, like a neutral commissioner. The issue was the pension plan, on which the owners were attempting to perpetrate a routine swindle. At the time, the plan provided $50 a month at age fifty for former players with five years of major-league service. Ten-year men got $100. Most of the financing came from the players themselves, particularly from their radio and television money. Previously, the license fees paid by radio and TV networks for the right to broadcast World Series games had gone to the players. This revenue had now been diverted to the pension fund, along with radio and TV payments for broadcasts of All-Star games. With the rapid enlargement of radio payments and the emergence of television as a bonanza, the owners decided to find other means of financing the retirement fund. Having established the plan unilaterally, without bargaining of any kind, they felt free to modify it at will. Above all, they felt free to keep the radio and TV money for themselves. This disturbed the players. They wondered if the plan was as permanent and stable as pension plans were supposed to be. They did not dare assert their rights, being uncertain as to whether they had rights. Yet it seemed to them that money already invested in the plan was their property and should be protected.

At this juncture, Commissioner Chandler went to bat for the hired hands. He announced publicly that he had been involved in the pension scheme from the beginning and that the original intent had been to earmark the radio and TV money for that purpose. He implied that the owners were trying to welch. As far as I know, this was the only occasion on which any Commissioner of Baseball has ever permitted facts to undermine his relationship with the owners. In 1951, Chandler was replaced by Ford C. Frick, a former newspaper columnist and radio commentator, who served the owners with unquestionable loyalty for more than thirteen years.

Continued uncertainty about the financing of the pension plan, and the players' equity in it, led in 1953 to a small insurrection, which the owners mistook for riot and civil disorder. Ralph Kiner was then the chief player representative for the National League. Allie Reynolds was his counterpart in the American League. Both were decent young men. Each believed himself responsible to the players he represented. It was a difficult situation. Could Kiner and Reynolds advocate the players' rights without offending the owners? Indeed, could they defend the players' rights without first finding out if the players had any rights?

In July 1953, Kiner and Reynolds met in Cincinnati with

Commissioner Frick and the two league presidents, Warren C. Giles and Will Harridge. They asked about the
pension financing. They asked whether the minimum salary
might not be raised above $5,000. They suggested that
baseball would improve if players were not forced to play
doubleheaders on days immediately following night games.
They submitted that it was exhaustingly difficult to go
directly from a night game to the airport or railroad station
and play another game in another city on the following
afternoon. The response was discouraging. Though Frick
and the others were the top functionaries of baseball, they
stated that none of these matters could be dealt with at
the meeting. Consideration might be given later, in more
appropriate yet undefined settings, but no date could be
specified, nor could the ultimate decisions be forecast. The
brush-off was customary but this time it didn't work.

In August, Reynolds disclosed to the press that he and
Kiner had retained the services of J. Norman Lewis, a
lawyer. Lewis confirmed this. "I will merely be a legal guide
for the players," he said mildly, in case anyone thought
he was planning to upset applecarts.

Holy cow! By hiring a lawyer you'd think the players
had fired on Fort Sumter.

George Weiss (Yankees): "I can't believe it, maybe
because I don't want to believe it. It certainly doesn't
sound like something Allie Reynolds would do."

Gabe Paul (Reds): "We've never before had any difficulties with our players and don't anticipate any."

Warren Giles (National League): "The players can do
more for themselves than any outside representatives. . . .
If the players delegate to anyone outside their own ranks
any of these rights to discuss and negotiate individually,
they are surrendering a privilege that has been very valuable
to them."

Frank Lane (White Sox): "I asked Reynolds who was going to pay for the lawyer. He told me he thought the owners would. . . ."

J. Norman Lewis: "You can say this for me. It definitely is not my intention or plan to form any player union. This is a voluntary organization of players, trying to reach an agreement by amicable means."

Reynolds and Kiner: "Our main aim is to improve the relationship between the players and owners."

Kiner: "As far as I am concerned, I don't know anything of a serious nature that is bothering anyone."

Kiner and Reynolds took their lawyer to a meeting of the owners' executive council—Frick, Giles, Harridge, Walter O'Malley (Dodgers) and Tom Yawkey (Red Sox). The council refused to see Lewis. He sat in the hall. But some kind of understanding must have been achieved. A few days later, Lewis reiterated that no union was being formed. He said that he was perfectly content to abide by the owners' wishes, as far as meetings were concerned. If the owners chose, he would meet with Frick, Harridge and Giles. He had no anger or bitterness in him.

In September, the executive council met again, this time with Kiner, Reynolds and J. Norman Lewis. An official communique reported that the players "had achieved more in the five-hour discussion than in the previous eight years." Here are the assurances the players got:

1. More money to defray the moving expenses of a traded player.

2. Payment of the full hotel rate to players who lived away from the team hotel during spring training.

3. Payment by clubs of the player's surgical expenses, even if the illness or injury was not incurred on the field.

4. Daily meal money of $8 while on road trips.

5. No improvement in the pension plan.

6. No change in the $5,000 minimum salary, although the council would discuss a $7,200 minimum with the owners.

In February 1954, a new pension-financing plan was announced by a committee that consisted of Kiner, Reynolds, Lewis, John W. Galbreath, owner of the Pirates, and Hank Greenberg, general manager of the Cleveland Indians. Beginning in 1957, the fund would be financed with 60 percent of baseball's income from radio and television broadcasts of World Series and All-Star games, plus 60 percent of the All-Star box-office receipts. Considering the determination to rock no boats, the new plan was a victory for the players. Greenberg thought so when Galbreath told him what the plan would be. Kiner and Reynolds thought so when Greenberg relayed the word.

Under the guidance of J. Norman Lewis, the affairs of the Major League Baseball Players Association became orderly, the meetings more substantive. The owners were dependable as ever about reneging on agreements previously arrived at, but the Association was now less resigned to such whims as a way of life. Excerpts from minutes of player representatives' meetings show what was going on:

September 30, 1957: "It was the general understanding that Commissioner Frick had assured Mr. Lewis that all clubs would pay . . . players who live . . . outside of the hotel the same sum of money that the club would have to pay if the player resided in the hotel. However, this situation did not seem to prevail in the Washington club, and Mr. Lewis was requested to take the matter up with Commissioner Frick. . . ."

July 6, 1959: "Bob Feller reported that he wished to stress to the players the importance of the 60–40 guarantee

. . . relative to the revenue for the pension fund. He also stressed the importance of public opinion and that the players did not wish to create an impression of a 'money grab,' but at the same time had to be extra-cautious regarding the owners fulfilling their obligation on the 60–40 split."

Talk of that kind may seem tame to the reader. But it thundered like heavy artillery in the ears of the owners, whose agents in the Association informed them of its every move. The minimum salary had been raised to $6,000. Plumbing had been repaired in clubhouses. Splinterless benches had been installed in dugouts. Yet these player representatives continued to hold their subversive meetings and send their spokesman around with impudent requests. To them, the lawyer had become a gadfly.

Lewis was not happy, either. His relationship with the players took a great deal of time and energy, and was unremunerative. Discussions about making him counsel to the pension fund proved fruitless. The owners would not agree. In 1960, therefore, Lewis was replaced by Judge Robert C. Cannon, of the Wisconsin Circuit Court, under whose direction the policies and practices of the Association returned to normal. Which is to say that the Association stopped giving owners a hard time. The owners were pleased. Many players were not. Yet, six years of Judge Cannon taught them a great deal more about the facts of baseball life.

If the Judge differed with the owners on any issue of fundamental importance to us employees, we never learned where the disagreement lay. Under his guidance, our Association agreed to prolong the season from 154 to 162 games. In return, we got a $2 increase in the daily food allowance. Our pension plan also suffered a few setbacks, one of which—as we learned much later—engaged the attention of the New York State Insurance Department. I'll come to that shortly.

Cannon made his debut at a player-rep meeting in December 1959. According to the minutes, he emphasized that "a harmonious existence between players and owners should be the purpose of all." He was always very big on the Good of the Game. He worked for us without formal compensation, except for a $15,000-a-year expense stipend, which came at first from the pension committee and later from the Association itself.

Before he had been in office a year, a movement was afoot to establish a permanent, full-time Association headquarters. The judge would move in. His functions as our legal advisor would expand to include administrative duties in the pension fund. Association minutes suggest that financing for this move was expected from the owners. The minutes give no indication that anybody understood that such an arrangement would carry this company union to new heights of sweetheartism. Evidently, no one suspected that it might be illegal for an Association to accept payment from the employers or—as later was decided—from the pension fund.

During 1960, a few of the more alert player representatives were eager to obtain a written agreement binding the owners to the pension-financing arrangement negotiated by Lewis, Kiner and Reynolds. These players feared that the owners might change their minds about allowing 60 percent of all that radio and television swag to become part of a pension fund. No confrontation occurred, however. Having received what he described as verbal "assurances" from Commissioner Ford Frick, Judge Cannon saw no basis for alarm. Beginning in 1961, the owners permitted Cannon to sit on the committee that administered the pension plan.

In 1961, this pension committee decided that the owners had contributed $167,440 more than necessary during 1960. The money was refunded, an act of generosity that later caused a sensation in the office of the New York State Department of Insurance. One of the state examiners made the point that the pension fund had been raped and pension laws violated.

Obviously, there had been no unlawful intent. The money had been refunded overzealously by partisans of the Good of the Game. I am not being completely facetious. In those days, the Association's primary problem was ignorance of the broad principles that govern fairness in employer-employee relationships. Whatever we had, we owed to the employer with abject gratitude. Whatever else we might get could be obtained only though his paternal kindness. He was a feudal lord and we were his humble petitioners.

The pension rebate occurred because radio and television revenues had increased. The pension plan's benefits were so modest that the 1960 remittances from the owners had been larger than required. This meant that some of the clubs could not lawfully deduct their entire pension contributions from taxes. Galbreath, Greenberg, Kiner, Reynolds and Lewis had provided for such an eventuality. Stipulating that only tax-deductible contributions could be made to the fund, their original agreement had prescribed various methods of making sure that all contributions would be deductible. To refund money to the owners violated the agreement.

The pension committee could have liberalized the pension or health benefits of the plan sufficiently to absorb the extra $167,440, making the money tax-deductible. Or the additional money could have been contributed to the Association of Professional Baseball Players (a charity for old-timers). A third alternative would have added the extra money to the players' share of World Series proceeds. But the committee decided to overlook these mandates of the pension plan. It decided to be considerate and give the owners a rebate.

In 1962, the major leagues expanded. Instead of sixteen teams, there were now twenty. The number of active players encompassed by the plan increased by 25 percent. The pension committee might well have altered the funding provisions to meet these increased expenses. But it did not. The players themselves were saddled with the increased costs of insurance coverage. Meanwhile, network telecasting had expanded to include the popular "Game of the Week." The considerable revenue from this feature was retained by the owners. Not a dime of it went to the pension fund. The Association presented no obstacle to this decision. And Happy Chandler was long gone.

The Association was not reorganized until 1966. If we players had understood what was going on during 1960 and 1961 and 1962, we might have taken strong measures sooner than we did. But understanding was in short supply. Except for a handful of conscientious player representatives, most of whom were led around by the nose, we all gave the Association less attention than it deserved. We expected nothing good of it. To some of the more worldly among us it was a stooge organization right out of the employer's hip pocket. It was just one more item on our long list of grumbles.

When Bob Howsam, briefly the general manager of the Cardinals, appointed Tim McCarver and me the co-captains of the team, I was afraid that I would have to become the player representative and go to Association meetings. I was delighted when Tim was awarded that chore. By all accounts, the meetings were dreary affairs in which the players listened passively to Judge Cannon's dissertations on the Good of the Game. Little time was expended on basic issues. The largest issue of all, the reserve system, is not even mentioned in the minutes of that period. The Association spent its time on its hands and knees, trying to wheedle the owners into abiding by agreements concerning an endlessly repetitive and self-replenishing assortment of problems, some of which were not entirely trivial but none of which approached the real difficulties of the players.

Robin Roberts, Jim Bunning, Harvey Kuenn and a few other leaders were convinced that the Association would benefit from the long-standing plan to establish a permanent office with a full-time executive director. The owners agreed. Moreover, they agreed that the office and its staff should be underwritten with money from the pension fund. It was taken for granted by all parties that Judge Cannon was the logical choice for the new position.

Cannon displayed some hesitancy about quitting the bench. Also, it became known that several owners considered him a likely successor to Ford Frick as Commissioner of Baseball. Roberts and his colleagues began looking elsewhere for possible executive directors. Late in 1965, Roberts consulted Dr. George Taylor, chairman of the Economics Department at the University of Pennsylvania's Wharton School of Finance. Taylor, an expert on labor relations, recommended that the players interview Marvin J. Miller, the chief economic advisor to the United Steelworkers of America and assistant to the union's president. Miller agreed to accept the job, if nominated by the Association's executive board and elected in a referendum of all players.

The player representatives met during January 1966 and nominated Judge Cannon by a narrow margin over Miller, Bob Feller and three other candidates. As nearly as anyone could tell, the Association's future was now assured. Smooth relations with the owners would continue uninterrupted. Robin Roberts' adventures in the outside world had come to naught. Baseball was still baseball, an unopened clam.

But accidents do happen. A few hours after his nomination, Judge Cannon upset Bob Friend, of the Pittsburgh Pirates, who had been among his staunch advocates. He disclosed to Friend that he harbored certain misgivings about the proposed arrangement. The Association office should be in Milwaukee or Chicago, he said, rather than in New York as the players intended. Furthermore, if he were to quit the bench, some sort of pension would have to be devised for him.

At this juncture, Bob Friend became a supporter of the defeated Marvin Miller. The fact that the nomination had already been decided and recorded meant absolutely nothing. Baseball players had never been slaves of parliamentary procedure. Beginning with the first strike vote taken in Pittsburgh in 1946, and continuing without hindrance ever since, decisions solemnly arrived at by vote had been reversed just as solemnly in second votes. Accordingly, Friend now asked Marvin Miller if he would accept the nomination. The economist was startled. He felt like a tourist in the Land of Oz. Where he came from, decisions were more durable. After collecting himself, he replied that he could accept the nomination only if Cannon withdrew publicly. Shortly thereafter, Cannon did so. The player representatives reconvened and nominated Miller. Baseball had crossed the threshold of a new era.

To introduce himself to the ball players and give them some conception of what the upcoming referendum was all about, Miller toured the training camps early in 1966. Wherever he went, a campaign of invidious opposition

preceded him. Postcards, telephone calls, leaflets and newspaper articles reminded the players that baseball could not
survive an attack of "labor bossism." The two league presidents, Joe Cronin and Warren Giles, were prominent in
the campaign. So was Lee MacPhail, an emissary from the
office of General William D. Eckert, who had succeeded
Ford Frick as Commissioner. Judge Cannon, who had
come within hailing distance of Eckert's job, also expressed
dismay about Miller.

It was suggested that Miller might deliver the ball players
to the Mafia. And that the players would be forced to pay
exorbitant dues. And that individual bargaining would be
replaced with collectivistic wage formulas by means of
which the minimum salary would become the maximum.
After his years in the hard-won sophistication of the modern
labor movement, poor Miller had been teleported back to
the Stone Age.

Arriving in Los Angeles during his tour, he saw headlines
beneath which Joe Adcock, Bob Rodgers and Jack Sanford
of the local Angels were quoted as agreeing, "We don't
want a labor boss." Miller was flabbergasted. Rodgers was
one of the player representatives—a member of the govern-
ing body that had voted to nominate him. Marvin phoned
Bob to inquire about the change of heart. The conversation
revealed much about the self-defeating procedures in which
Association leaders had been trained.

"What goes on?" asked Miller. "The player reps voted
for me."

"You don't understand," replied Bob earnestly. "I have
to represent my players and their views."

"But they don't know me," protested Miller. "They
haven't met me. You have. What is the responsibility of
leadership in a situation of this kind?"

"You just don't understand," insisted Bob. "That isn't

the way it works!" He later became a forceful leader of the Association.

At a players' meeting in the hotel of a team that Miller prefers not to identify in print, the discussion was constructive and enlightening until the team manager took the floor and began firing hostile questions at Marvin. The manager wanted to know whether Miller was planning a strike. And under what circumstances he would order a strike. And for what purposes. And would the players be taking orders from outsiders. Miller finally silenced the man by pointing out that this was a meeting of players and could not be devoted entirely to the concerns of the management. Two years later, when the manager inevitably had become a former manager, he looked up Miller and apologized. "Sometimes a man has to do things that he doesn't want to do," he explained. "I had my orders."

When he visited the Cardinals, Marvin impressed us as a calm, self-possessed, thoroughly reasonable man with a broader grasp of our problems than any of us had. We had been sent our share of anti-Miller propaganda, but, as I recall saying at the time, "If the owners are so vehemently opposed to the guy, he can't be too bad." He won the referendum by a vote of 489 to 136. The Cleveland Indians gave him only one vote. The Giants gave him none. Majorities on the California Angels and Chicago Cubs also voted against him.

After the referendum, the owners got desperate. Lee MacPhail actually advised the player representatives to save the sport by refusing to sign Marvin Miller's contract. At about the same time, the owners let it be known that they no longer could agree to the establishment of an Association headquarters financed by pension contributions. Commissioner Eckert called a special meeting of the player representatives to explain why.

"You are not invited," he told Miller.

"This is curious," answered Marvin. "The owners whom you represent have reneged on their agreement that an Association office could be financed out of the players' moneys in the pension fund. We all know that I am the reason why they changed their minds. And now you actually expect to meet the players without me?"

"I am the Commissioner," observed the Commissioner. "I must do as I see fit."

"Very well, Commissioner," said Miller. "If you exclude the Association's elected executive director from the meeting, there may be no meeting."

No Commissioner of Baseball had ever been challenged so directly by a spokesman for players. After consulting with his employers about the advisability of a public squabble over the players' right to choose their own executive director, General Eckert retreated. Miller attended the meeting. So did a platoon of baseball bigwigs and attorneys. The proceedings were stenographically recorded. Various members of the owners' delegation complained that the original notion of an Association headquarters had differed somehow from what was now contemplated. Paul Porter, the law associate of Thurman Arnold and Abe Fortas, finally pointed out in behalf of the owners that any arrangement to divert pension moneys to the upkeep of the Association would be illegal. And had been illegal from the beginning. The implication was clear enough. The illegality had not become noticeable until the character of the Association had begun to change.

We had been educated, most of us, to regard labor organizations as devices for the personal aggrandizement of labor leaders. To this day, the press tends to depict the affairs of the Major League Baseball Players Association as a series of skirmishes between Marvin J. Miller and the owners.

Nothing could be further from the truth. Among Miller's first priorities was the establishment of democratic procedures unprecedented in our experience. Reports from player reps and detailed memorandums from the Association itself kept rank-and-file members informed of all issues, all developments. Miller's success as a negotiator rests only partly on his skill and experience. Marvin's real strength lies in the owners' awareness that he is spokesman for the demands of an informed constituency.

At the start he was virtually alone in understanding this elementary truth about the effectiveness of voluntary organizations. But baseball players are not stupid. They liked his approach, and learned from it. Let me quote from the minutes of Marvin's first meeting, in which he cast new light on the Association's traditional goal of seeking harmony with the owners:

"The problem of developing an appropriate, constructive relationship with the owners was discussed. Mr. Miller commented that on his visits to the twenty training camps . . . he had been told by the players on about half of the clubs that the relationship with the owners was good. The other half indicated some dissatisfaction. He said that a 'good relationship' was very easy to attain and maintain when there were no problems, or when one party to a relationship either did not ask for anything or accepted repeated rebuffs. The test of a good relationship lies, in part, in the results attained. He said that the history of relationships between the players and owners was somewhat at variance with the picture presented by some. Some players apparently believe that certain of the benefits enjoyed by the players was gracefully presented with no effort on the part of the players. In fact, a great deal of effort and determination was required to obtain significant advances. . . . Mr. Miller said it was clear that the players were interested in having an effective Association . . . and that the most important factor was player support. He emphasized that this did not mean unquestioning acceptance, but rather full debate and discussion and then full support of decisions arrived at democratically."

Players who heard that speech reported that their horizons widened on the spot. Not only did players have rights, but they had the means of exercising their rights. It was a whole new ball game. And we had a strong feeling that it would be played with integrity. For example, Miller told that first big meeting that he was going to itemize his working expenses and collect exact reimbursement, instead of accepting lump sums without such accounting, as had been the previous practice.

The organization was now financed by dues. Less than 1 percent of the players refused to pay them. As of 1969, by the way, only one player was not an Association member. This was an aging pitcher who had become an enthusiastic booster of Association policies and methods.

"Why should I pay dues when I only have another season or two left?" he asked with a logic so appealingly frugal that nobody really minded.

The revamped Association was effective from the very beginning. In this respect, the owners were a tremendous help. They fortified our sense of purpose by continuing the shenanigans that had precipitated our uprising in the first place. At the very moment when we were signing voluntary authorizations for the deduction of dues from our paychecks, some newspapers denounced the Association for demanding compulsory dues. The misinformation could have come from only one source. And in August 1966, when the owners announced that they had decided to stop contributing 60 percent of certain radio and television moneys to our benefit plan, some of the same reporters accused *us* of unconscionable greed.

Our anger drew us closer together. Our new knowledge

of our own affairs made us more formidable bargainers. We now knew, for example, that the benefit plan was a matter for negotiation and should not be dictated by the owners. Led by Marvin Miller and the Association's new counsel, Richard M. Moss, our negotiating committee managed to retain for us a 60 percent share of the radio and TV receipts, meanwhile modernizing the plan dramatically. Our advisors knew how to produce larger pension benefits per premium dollar than had seemed possible in the bad old days. The plan now covers all aspects of our health care, including dentistry, and provides retirement benefits at age fifty that range from $240 a month for a player with four years of service to $800 a month for a twenty-year man. A four-year player who defers his benefits until the age of sixty is entitled to $447.63 a month, or at sixty-five he can get $618.04. Ten-year men get $600 a month at fifty, $1,119.07 if they wait until sixty, and $1,545.11 at sixty-five. And the twenty-year man gets $1,452.07 at sixty and $1,945.11 at sixty-five.

In 1968, a new basic wage contract was signed after more than a year of unbelievably bitter maneuvering. Here again the owners got our backs up and made us fight. For eleven years, the minimum salary had been $6,000—unchanged throughout eleven years of inflation. In December 1966, we proposed that the minimum be increased to $12,000. We made numerous other proposals intended to introduce a measure of reasonableness into employer-player relations. For months, the owners refused to bargain. They finally agreed to receive our committee (Steve Hamilton of the Yankees, Jim Pagliaroni of the Pirates, Marvin Miller and Dick Moss) at a meeting of the club general managers in Fort Lauderdale, Florida, during March 1967.

When our men arrived, no general managers or owners were to be seen. Instead, President Joe Cronin of the American League turned up with someone from the National League and a couple of lawyers. They announced that they had come not to talk but to listen. They were true to their word. They refused to comment on our proposals. They offered none of their own. When our committee urged them to negotiate, they said, repeatedly, that it would "serve no useful purpose."

In former years, an incident of that kind would not have been reported to the rank and file. But we learned promptly of what had happened at Fort Lauderdale. And we were kept informed of developments throughout the 1967 season, during which the owners obstinately refused to negotiate. More players than ever became Association-conscious. Fewer and fewer were deluded by baseball's paternalism.

The last straw was laid on in Mexico City during November. A negotiation session scheduled for St. Louis had been canceled. In Mexico, the owners would talk turkey at last. Marvin Miller, Dick Moss and player representatives from each club arrived hopefully. I think I should name the player reps. They belong in history, as men who educated themselves rapidly enough to lead the rest of us through the intensely difficult changes of that period. They were Jack Aker (Athletics), Max Alvis (Indians), Jim Bunning (Pension Committee), Roberto Clemente (Pirates), Don Drysdale (Dodgers), Jack Fisher (Mets), Bill Freehan (Tigers), Dave Giusti (Astros), Dick Hall (Phillies), Tom Haller (Giants), Steve Hamilton (Yankees), Bob Humphreys (Senators), Randy Hundley (Cubs), Dave Johnson (Orioles), Bob Locker (White Sox), Tim McCarver (Cardinals), Dave Morehead (Red Sox), Russ Nixon (Twins), Milt Pappas (Reds), Bob Rodgers (Angels), and Joe Torre (Braves). All of them had been properly elected by their teammates. Faced with undeniable facts, all proved solid citizens who cared, really cared, about the well-being of their fellow professionals.

I spoke of the last straw. The next-to-last straw came

when the owners would not set a time for the meeting. Miller and his men were advised to cool their heels and await further word. They got small satisfaction from the printed agenda of the owners' own meeting, which indicated that a period had been set aside for discussions with the Association. The minutes of a meeting held by the Association's Executive Board (the men named above), show the effect that all this was having.

"Several of the Board members expressed their opinion that the basic problem of the relationship between the club owners and the players as a group is the same as it has always been; that the owners (or, at least, the majority of them) have no reluctance to turn down even the most reasonable of proposals since they proceed on the theory that the players will do nothing about it if they just say 'no'; and that we will continue to make a minimum of progress, both in these negotiations and in next year's negotiation on the Benefit Plan, unless we can somehow demonstrate to the owners that times have changed, that the players are intent on receiving appropriate compensation, benefits and working conditions for their professional efforts, and that, if need be, they will take affirmative action to secure that result."

Now the last straw. The owners' collective bargaining expert, John Gaherin (who had performed similar functions for the New York Newspaper Publishers Association), announced that the negotiating meeting was off. The owners were too busy, he said.

Miller and his board called in the press and reviewed the history of the negotiations. Whereupon the owners called a press conference of their own. Chief spokesman was Joe Cronin, who denied that a negotiations session had been scheduled. Paul Richards, the guiding genius of the Atlanta Braves, offered choice remarks of his own. The burden of his observations was that Marvin Miller had introduced a note of unseemliness into the national pastime. "Somebody's lying," said Richards soberly. "And I don't think it's the owners. If this guy continues this kind of tactics, I guess we'll just have to get in the gutter with him."

Cooler heads ultimately prevailed. The establishment's performance had been so transparent and so widely publicized, and the players had reacted with such dignity, that the Image of the Game became more threadbare than ever. Negotiations finally began in November and concluded in February 1968 with the first written agreement between the Association and the owners. The minimum salary was raised to $10,000. Murphy money, which had been $25 for each week of spring training since 1947, now became $40. On-the-road food allowances were increased. First-class hotel and travel accommodations became contractual requirements. And, for the first time in the history of baseball, a procedure for the orderly resolution of grievances was established.

It was not much of a grievance procedure, because its final stage was arbitration by the Commissioner of Baseball. As Dick Moss said in a speech to the Federal Bar Association, "The Commissioner is hired by, paid by and can be fired by the club owners. I know [the grievance procedure] sounds shameful, but that was the best we could do."

Which reminds me of what happened to Rico Carty. Playing winter baseball in the Dominican Republic, he got into a rhubarb with an umpire who had called him out in a close play at second base. During the debate, Rico bumped the umpire—accidentally, he says. He was then ejected from the field and fined $50. Weeks later, he got a telegram from Bowie K. Kuhn, the lawyer who succeeded General Eckert as Commissioner of Baseball. The wire informed Rico that Kuhn had raised the fine to $500 "after

reviewing the case." This review had included no opportunity for Carty to present his own side of the story. Indeed, Rico had not even known that a review was taking
place. Some review! If the player had decided to make a
contractual grievance of the matter, it would have been
settled by Kuhn—the very pasha against whom the grievance would have been filed.

In 1970, the Association won a contract which provides
that all grievances may be resolved by impartial arbitration,
except in cases that involve the "integrity of the game."
It remains to be seen how the owners and Kuhn will
interpret "integrity of the game." But I am ahead of my
story.

On September 30, 1968, preparing for gory renegotiation
of the benefit plan, the Association's Executive Board resolved unanimously that players should not sign their 1969
contracts until the membership had ratified a new plan.
With exceptions too few to matter, the players stood fast.
An improved system of retirement, health and other insurance benefits was worked out. We had finally showed
our guts. It was a great feeling. The owners had begun by
insisting that no agreement could be made unless we (a)
relinquished all claim to a right in radio and television
revenue, (b) conceded that the benefit plan could be terminated at will by the owners, and (c) excluded all former
players from improved benefits.

Somehow, the owners got the impression from Bowie
Kuhn that the Association had agreed to surrender the
players' rights to the radio and TV money. When this
proved untrue, the owners assumed that we had double-
crossed them. A good deal of bitterness arose. The Association had begged the owners to sit in on negotiating sessions
to learn what was going on, but they preferred to abstain.
More than once, we learned that our arguments were losing

something in Kuhn's translation to the absent owners. On the other hand, the owners were convinced that their professional bargainers were doing a dandy job, an idea that the negotiators did nothing to contradict. We found out about these goings-on when our separate club owners began chewing out individual players for acts of duplicity that neither we nor our Association had committed.

At any rate, we finally got the best pension plan in any sport. And Bowie Kuhn had established himself as a stout defender of the Integrity of the Game. From the players' point of view, he was straight Establishment, a grinder of the owners' ax. He differed from his predecessors in no important particular, unless it is significant to be more aggressive than Ford Frick and more lucid than General Eckert. In Appendix A to this book is a faithful summary of a dialogue that occurred between Kuhn and Association leaders at our meeting in Puerto Rico during December 1969. It is required reading for anyone who cares to know where impartiality and objectivity stand in the priorities assigned to the Commissioner of Baseball by those who pay his salary.

Having persuaded all concerned that it enjoyed the militant loyalty of an overwhelming majority of big-league players, the Association did not bother with a strike threat in negotiating its basic contract for the 1970 season. The instrument was signed for a three-year term. It included an increased minimum salary of $12,000 in 1970 and $13,500 in 1972. Murphy money rose to $50 a week. A severance pay arrangement compensated players released during spring training. In 1972, that clause will be strengthened to guarantee a full year's salary to any player released on or after May 15. The new arbitration clause was adopted.

No headway was made in the Association's attempts to negotiate some sense into the so-called reserve clause. In the previous basic agreement, the owners had contracted to join the Association in a study of "possible alternatives to the reserve clause." Not a thing had happened. The Association had submitted numerous ideas for discussion. Each had been greeted with total silence, save for an occasional flat no. Clearly, the reserve system would remain inviolate, and ball players would remain chattels until somebody did something special. The Association's leaders were all aware of this in 1966 and 1967 and 1968 and 1969. A strike on the issue was as yet premature. And, as yet, no player had demonstrated readiness to stake his own career in a court test.

11

If He Hollers

In 1967 we won the championship of the National League and defeated Boston in the World Series. In 1968 we won the championship of the National League and failed by one game to defeat Detroit in the World Series. In 1969 we lost the championship of the National League on March 22, before the season started.

August A. Busch, Jr., horseman, yachtsman, beer magnate and proprietor of the Cardinals, is the most baronial of major-league club owners. He also has the shortest fuse. During the 1969 pension negotiations, the Major League Baseball Players Association had offended his sense of propriety. We had refused to sign our individual salary contracts until the owners agreed to a better retirement plan. When they attempted to sever the traditional link between the pension fund and the sport's television and radio income, we had accused them, not unreasonably, of wanting to keep the receipts for themselves. After the negotiations ended in an acceptable compromise, the leading members of the Cardinals added injury to insult. They demanded substantial salary increases. I, for one, did not sign my contract until March 3—having been an official holdout for two brave days. I had rejected a $77,500 offer.

"If you people want a three-hundred hitter who also happens to be the best center fielder in baseball," I said with becoming modesty, "it will cost you ninety thousand dollars, which is not seventy-seven-five and is not eighty-nine thousand, nine hundred and ninety-nine." I got it. Bob Gibson, Lou Brock, Tim McCarver and several others also did handsomely. Mr. Busch's player payroll became the highest in the industry.

He had a fit. Profanity rattled the windows and turned the air blue (it is possible to be baronial and earthy at one and the same time). Labor annoyances were not what he had envisioned when he took up baseball. They could not be classified as wholesome sport. They were no fun at all. They boded ill for the future of the game. What would become of the fans? The fans! Mr. Busch decided to attack us in behalf of the fans. Accordingly, Mr. Busch staged a happening. He ordered all the Cardinals to a special meeting on March 22 at St. Petersburg, our Florida training base. He summoned the corporate directors of his beer and baseball enterprises. He whistled up the gentlemen of the press. When all had assembled, he addressed himself to the players.

He questioned the integrity of our attitudes. He raised doubts as to the single-mindedness of our professional efforts. He accused us of upstaging and occasionally manhandling our devoted fans. He deplored the methods of our Association. He warned that failure to mend our ways would ruin St. Louis baseball. He depicted us as a rabble of ingrates headed for a fall. Having humiliated us to the best of his ability, he exhorted us to go forth and win another pennant.

Although it was difficult to single out one part of the long speech as more offensive than others, I feel that Mr. Busch exceeded himself with these words:

> I do believe I have an obligation to remind you that this year, instead of talking baseball all during the off-season, most fans have had a steady diet of strike talk and dollar signs.
>
> I hope that is all behind us now. It has to be behind us. Too many fans are saying our players are getting fat—that they now only think of money—and less of the game itself. . . .
>
> Fans are telling us now that if we intend to raise prices to pay for the high salaries and so on and on, they will stop coming to the games, they will not watch and will not listen. They say they can do other things with their time and with their money.
>
> It doesn't take a crystal ball, gentlemen, to realize that with so many fans being so aware of the big payrolls in baseball, they will become more and more critical of us.

Picture the situation. If those remarks had been made by a stranger in a bar, any of the Cardinals would have felt free to reply and would have had no trouble exposing the mean reasoning for what it was. An answer would have emphasized that baseball players' salaries are low, not high. Baseball players' salaries compare unfavorably with those of other athletic performers, like golfers, basketball players and boxers, most of whom are paid far higher percentages of the gross. If baseball's customers are unhappy about the increasing salaries of players, it is because the baseball industry has promoted that peculiar frame of mind through the press.

But the remarks were not delivered by a stranger in a bar. The orator was the boss himself. His chief lieutenants were at his side. Reporters were covering the event. In no other industry of the Western world could an employer publicly belittle his professional staff without risking mass resignations. Knowing that we would not resign (because baseball law does not permit us to seek another employer), Busch was using the occasion not only to revile us but to reassert the uniquely feudal privileges vested in him and other club owners by baseball's reserve system.

The speech demoralized the 1969 Cardinals. The employer had put us in our place. Despite two successive pennants, we were still livestock. Proud of ourselves and our skills, we had assumed that the feeling permeated the front office as well. In fact, we had heard with some amusement that Busch himself was not above taking credit for certain of our achievements. But now it was over. Our Association had alerted Busch to matters of more abiding importance than the pennants we had won and the pennants that might await us. As his speech demonstrates, his primary goal was to whip us into line and keep us there. From the standpoint of the baseball industrialist, that is the name of the game.

His statement was printed and widely circulated as an example of corporate foresight, vision and courage. I offer the full text in Appendix B of this book. It deserves a close reading.

After he had finished, Busch asked if there were any questions. We had none. Reporters then moved among us in quest of comment. We kept silent. Any of us could have gained favor by pretending that the oratory had inspired the team to seek even greater heights in 1969 than in the past. But that would have been too shameful a lie even for baseball players, accustomed though they are to going along with the fantasies of the employer and the public. Yet, to tell reporters the truth—that the baron had been wrong— would have been to defy the very conventions that the whole ill-conceived meeting had been designed to reinforce. Busch had been talking to us in code. He had been telling us to behave or get out. I no longer felt like a $90,000 ball player but like a green recruit. I feared that if I so much as hinted at the truth about that meeting I would be gone from the team in a week. I was sick with shame and so was everyone else on the Cardinals except Busch and his claque.

A few days later, the front office underlined the message and completed the havoc by trading away our most popular player, Orlando Cepeda. He had symbolized the joyful togetherness of the champion Cardinals. In return for Cha-Cha, the Atlanta Braves sent us Joe Torre, a congenial man and an excellent player. But the glue was gone. We finished fourth in the National League's Eastern Division, thirteen games behind the upstart Mets. The great Cardinals were all washed up.

Before reviewing some of the occurrences that made my own departure from the Cardinals a foregone conclusion, I'd like to offer a few comments about baseball fans, for whose well-being August Busch professed such concern. Because fans are customers, the owners quite sensibly speak well of them. No statement from the Commissioner or a league president or a team's front office is complete without words of homage to those who buy tickets. The shrewd Mets have gone so far as to make each game an orgy of audience participation, allowing fans to carry placards and wave self-consciously at the television cameras. No harm done. The ceremonial recitations of players being interviewed on radio or TV usually include expressions of awed appreciation for the team's supporters. Fair enough.

In actual practice, the industry treats its customers the

same as other industries treat theirs. That is, it treats them like customers, getting as much from them as the traffic will bear and giving them no more than it must. Because of baseball's privileged place in our culture, the traffic bears somewhat more than it might. I speak particularly of the concessions granted to club owners by local authorities. When an owner buys his franchise and makes the real estate deals and arranges the tax abatements and other boons that facilitate the construction of his new stadium, he does it all for the fans, he says. Local legislators and administrators describe their involvement in much the same way. Few politicians dare to be looked upon as antibaseball.

Yet a point is reached when the beloved fan becomes an unwanted customer and the owner-sportsman an unadorned entrepreneur. It happens repeatedly. The Milwaukee Braves abandon one of baseball's most lucrative franchises (having milked it ruthlessly for thirteen years) and move to Atlanta. What happens to the celebrated Milwaukee fans? They shift for themselves, that's what. The Dodgers leave Brooklyn for Los Angeles. The Giants leave New York for San Francisco. The Athletics leave Philadelphia for Kansas City and then migrate to Oakland. The Pilots leave Seattle for Milwaukee after one season. In each instance, the owner's heralded solicitude for the fans runs second to his appetite for profit.

It seems to me that baseball players understand fans. They understand they pay the bills. They understand that fans are entitled to common courtesy in public places. They also understand that they themselves are entertainers and, as such, are expected to promote the box office.

I have argued in locker rooms that baseball's publicists have encouraged fans to adopt forms of behavior that would be unacceptable elsewhere in the entertainment world. When an actor blows his lines, nobody dares to boo him, much less throw bottles at him and call him names. I have read about movie fans tearing the clothes off stars, but I suspect that most such incidents are staged, or at least encouraged, by press agents. In my own considerable experience among movie and theater people, I have noted enviously that members of the public generally treat them with deference. "I'm sorry," smiles my dear friend Judy Pace, "but I have time for only two autographs. I'd love to sign more, but I'm way behind schedule." And her admirers *ooh* and *aah* and think that she's a lovely and gracious lady, which happens to be the fact.

The ball player—as Mr. Busch's speech made plain—is differently situated. The fan's proprietary interest in the baseball team is allowed full expression in the fan's traffic with players. You step into the street from the clubhouse after a doubleheader and are required under the terms of your employment contract to stand there for an hour signing autographs. It is part of your job. On good days, you enjoy the adulation. On bad days, when you have batting troubles or a head cold or a complaining wife or an ailing child, you would prefer to excuse yourself. You do so at your peril. So you stand there and sign and get pencils poked in your eye and try to prevent kids from tearing your lapels. You submit because you seldom are brave enough not to. The fan gets nowhere when he complains to the front office about the high cereal content of the overpriced hot dogs, or the recent increase in the price of admission. But if he complains that Curt Flood refused to autograph a scorecard for his son, Curt Flood is called onto the carpet in a hurry. As to laying hands on fans, a complaint of Busch's, it is impossible not to defend oneself in a crowd.

Naturally, one runs into a different type of attention in restaurants and other public places. Some of them stalk your table, making sure that it is really you. Or, as occasionally happens, awaiting a sign of recognition, having met you at a Kiwanis luncheon eight years earlier.

"You don't remember me, do you?" he finally asks.

"Well, sir, I'm not sure," you say, putting down your fork.

"You signed a picture for my kid," he says.

"Of course!" you enthuse. "But I'm afraid the name escapes me."

"Brown," he grumbles.

"Brown!"

You rise and grasp his hand.

"Sam Brown," he adds grouchily.

"Sam Brown! Well I'll be damned! How have you been, Sam? How's your kid?"

"You didn't even remember me," he accuses, going back to his complaint.

"Well, gee, Sam, it sure has been good to see you again."

"Baseball stars! Big shots! Swellheads!" he snarls. Lord knows what you have done to the Image of the Game.

During the 1967 World Series, Charline and Bob Gibson and Judy Pace and I were having dinner in a Boston restaurant. A lady walked over, stalked a while and approached Bob.

"Bob Gibson!" she proclaimed.

He looked up from his plate.

"Mr. Gibson, I admire you so much! Sign this ticket for tomorrow's game?"

"Fine," said Bob. "Please permit me to eat my dinner. Then I'll be glad to sign your ticket."

She seemed pleased. She returned to her table and reported to her husband. I do not know what she told him, but the man grabbed her ticket, brought it to our table, tore it up and threw the pieces in Bob's face. He then rejoined his wife.

Bob did a slow burn. I could see the changes in his face. He rose, brushed off Charline's restraining hand, strode to the other table, put his face close to the man's and said, "Listen, you. I don't give a shit about you or your wife. This is my dinner time and right now I don't even give a shit about the World Series. I am not required to put up with you."

He came back to our table feeling much better and finished his meal. The other man was pale. It was better than he deserved.

"I don't have to take that," said Bob.

Amen. A baseball player's whole life depends on a keyed-up nervous system. He operates on a hair trigger. To touch him is like grabbing a cocked gun. If he is occasionally irritable in crowds, it is not unnatural. Do you suppose that the game would suffer if fans were told to approach players with some consideration?

Another side of our difficulties with fans is critically important. It involves the game's integrity. Ball players are forever being approached by angle-shooters looking for inside information, which they presumably use to make bets. How does the player differentiate between the curiosity of the faithful and the more purposeful questions of a gambler?

New York is infested with wise guys. They frequent the hangouts of ball players and manage to get into conversations: "Tell me like it is. How *is* Bob Gibson's arm? Will he be able to go another two–three years?"

The gambler hopes you will say something about Hoot's current condition, so that he can bet accordingly. Most players are wary enough to smell a gambler, get up and walk away. But you never really know to whom you are talking. Players, myself included, have been jumped on for brushing off innocent fans whom we suspected of scouting for bookies. We really don't care if someone cashes a bet on a baseball game, but we want no part of the action, obviously. Above all, we dare not be suspected of helping gamblers.

An interesting character known as Big Julie used to behave as if he owned our clubhouse in New York. A jovial, expansive fellow rumored to have important political connections, he introduced players to pretty women, bought lavish meals and otherwise ingratiated himself. He looked like a swifty to me, and I gave him a wide berth. Others said that he simply was a baseball buff with money to spend. That has always been a problem of mine, I guess— trying to figure out whether a new acquaintance wanted my friendship or simply hoped to be seen in public with an athlete, or was trying to promote information.

One night a couple of the players were out on the town with Big Julie. It was time for them to get back to the hotel. So they left wherever they were and walked to their host's car. When they had almost reached its parking place at the curb, Big Julie stepped into a doorway. The baffled ball players stood there while another man, supposedly a business associate of Julie's, got into the front seat and turned on the ignition. Big Julie then emerged from the doorway and climbed behind the wheel.

"What was that all about?" asked a ball player.

"Don't let it bother you, kid," said Big Julie.

"It doesn't exactly bother me," trembled the player, "but, I mean, why did you hide in the doorway while he started the motor for you?"

"Been having a few little arguments lately," advised Big Julie. "Needed to make sure that the car wasn't wired to blow up."

Further traffic with Big Julie was out. I did not see him in our locker room again. But I thought of him during 1970 when I read that Denny McLain had been suspended for half of the season, after *Sports Illustrated* revealed that he had invested in a bookmaking deal from which he never collected a nickel of profit.

After being reminded by August Busch that we had fewer reasons for professional pride than we had deluded ourselves into thinking, we Cardinals became a morose and touchy team. Our concentration suffered. So did the remarkable spirit of fraternity that had helped us dominate the league for two years in succession. We remained keen about each other as athletes and men, but the opposing team was no longer our chief adversary, nor was the next game the most important problem in our lives. Each of us was miserably aware that the ax was over our skulls, by proclamation of Mr. Busch. We no longer believed that we worked for the best organization in baseball, a relative accolade that the Cardinal management had earned by leaving its players pretty much to their own devices, paying them comparatively well and transporting them in comfort. Far from applauding what we had built for ourselves and our employer, the front office appreciated it not at all. Indeed, the front office was prepared to destroy what we had built. It was hellbent on reinstating conventional relations, which find the players in a constant state of terrified insecurity.

And so we began behaving like conventional baseball players. We grumbled and groused. For example, I had long been known throughout the league as an agitator against the doubleheader, the 162-game season and, most pointedly, the inequities of the reserve system. During 1969, I protested more vigorously than usual, and even broke into print a few times. This did not endear me to management. Especially not at $90,000 a year.

Times had changed. Where once my painting of oil portraits had been tolerated, even encouraged, it was now deplored. Implementing Busch's notion that some of us were not sufficiently dedicated, the front office nagged Lou Brock about his Dodge agency and flower shop, Nelson Briles about his electronics dealership, Hoot Gibson about his Omaha interests, Tim McCarver about his Memphis restaurant. I was the worst offender of the lot. Not only did I paint until all hours, but my name now was associated with a photography business. How could I be expected to keep my mind on baseball?

I'll tell you how. The major-league baseball player is even more aware of the perils of distraction than general managers and owners. He cannot excel unless his mind is on the game. He has known this since childhood. If he becomes involved in businesses outside baseball, he does so as an absentee partner. He usually invests little except the use of his name. His business affairs are attended to (not always honestly or efficiently) by the persons to whom he has lent his name. How could it be otherwise? He is on the road half the time, and tense with athletic concentration when at home. Why, then, does he involve himself in outside interests? Partly in hope of getting extra money. Mainly in hope that his brief prestige may help him to prepare a place for himself in the world. The likelihood is great that baseball will have no room for him after his playing days end. It is little more likely, I might add, that the outside business will prosper. But you can't blame a man for trying.

Another of Mr. Busch's scars had been inflicted when players demanded payment for certain radio and television interviews. The spring training camps are overrun with semiprofessional communicators, each bearing a tape recorder or a movie camera, or both. After getting under our feet for weeks, they return home and peddle the interviews for commercial use throughout the season. Since the stuff serves to sell detergents, automobiles and other merchandise in small towns, and does not usually promote ticket sales for the player's team, it seemed reasonable to us that we be paid for our performances.

After the owners summarily rejected a proposal to this effect from the players, it occurred to me that we could invoke the terms of our individual contracts to discourage all those interviews. Our contracts state that no player can appear on radio or television without written permission from his club. So we began sending the free lancers to the front office for written permissions. You'd have thought we were burning Old Glory. We were informed in no uncertain terms that these were not the kinds of television and radio appearances referred to in the contract. No, these were promotional undertakings for the betterment of the game. Did not our contracts require us to cooperate with the club in such activities? Our contracts certainly did. The incident must have rankled the front office even more profoundly than I realized, considering the emotion with which Busch resurrected it in his speech.

The tensest episodes of the 1969 season occurred toward its end. We still had a mathematical chance of winning in our division, but the front office had already given up on us. As the saying goes, they had decided to "build for the future." They ordered Red Schoendienst to begin using a couple of promising but raw youngsters as regulars. Joe Hague began playing first base and batting third. Ted Simmons, a catcher, batted fifth. I liked the kids but hated what was happening. With Hague batting third, Lou Brock and I—the first two batters in the order—would not see any decent pitches. The other teams would pitch around us—walk us, if necessary—to get at the kid. They then could pitch around the fourth man to get at the other kid. Since both Lou and I were struggling to get our averages up to .300, and had not yet abandoned all hope of winning the divisional title, I concluded that the front office was sabotaging us.

"They've already sold a million-and-a-half tickets this season," I ranted, "so they can well afford to prevent us from having good years. Wait and see how they rub it in at contract time next winter."

I went to Red Schoendienst and demanded, "If you insist on playing those goddamned kids, at least don't put them in the heart of your lineup."

Bland as ever, and as cooperative, he shrugged and replied, "Okay. If you feel that way. about it."

Red seemed relieved to have an excuse for changing the batting order. I knew in my bones that the experiment had been suggested by the front office, and now the feeling was confirmed. Angrier than before, I confided to Jack Herman, a reporter for the *Globe-Democrat*, that the top management had tossed in the towel for 1969. I went on at some length.

The next day, he published my views, attributing them to an unnamed veteran. Bing Devine, our general manager, responded with a crusher. "The only reason the regulars are complaining," he said, "is that they are afraid of losing their jobs."

I think I had known it for months without admitting it to myself. Now I said to me, "Brother Flood, you are going to be traded. You have had it."

To which I answered, "They would not dare!"

"Wanna bet?" I replied.

On October 8, I was sitting in my apartment, waiting

for my nervous system to come down to earth. The season
was over. I had finished with a batting average of .285,
which was below my usual standard. On the other hand,
only nineteen full-time players in the league had managed
higher averages. I had hit safely 173 times—eleventh in the
league. If only nine more batted balls had dropped in, I'd
have hit .300. Reveries of a baseball player. No wonder so
many of us drink during the off-season. No wonder so many
of us drink all year round.

In three days I would leave for Copenhagen, where I
could unwind in blissful anonymity. Europe enthralled me,
and Copenhagen was my favorite place. An all-night town,
Copenhagen, marvelous for its uncomplicated directness.
The Danes have never heard of baseball. A black face might
intrigue them, but it neither alarms nor dismays them.
Copenhagen was a poultice for my bruised, battered and
self-pitying soul. Johnny and Marian Jorgensen had told
me often that I would love the place. I had been there and
they had been right.

The telephone sounded.

"Hello, Curt?"

"Yes."

"Jim Toomey, Curt."

A chill entered my belly. Toomey was assistant to Bing
Devine in the front office.

"Curt, you've been traded to Philadelphia."

Silence.

"You, McCarver, Hoerner and Byron Browne. For
Richie Allen, Cookie Rojas and Jerry Johnson."

Silence.

"Good luck, Curt."

"Thanks. Thanks a lot."

Twelve years of my life. I spent the rest of the day in the

chair right next to the telephone, answering none of the calls. *Twelve years of my life.*

I said to Marian, "There ain't no way I'm going to pack up and move twelve years of my life away from here. No way at all."

12

Let Him Go

If I had taken inventory before the front office called, I would have compiled a formidable list. Expensive athlete. Painter of oil portraits as negotiable as any currency. Student of the human condition. Impervious to shock. Subdivision: black. Belief in the American dream: lapsed.

Wrong. The dream dies hard. It lay deep within me, dormant but not destroyed. Just as stress can arouse a latent virus, one miserable telephone call released the poison of self-pity. The hard-boiled realist who answered the telephone was a weeping child when he set the receiver down.

The lightning had struck. The dream lay shattered. It was a bad scene. Feverishly, I harped on my twelve years of service, my place among the all-time stars of the Cardinals. My batting average of .285 had not been bad for a losing year. If I had been a foot-shuffling porter, they might have at least given me a pocket watch. But all I got was a call from a middle-echelon coffee drinker in the front office.

Was I not entitled to a gesture from the general manager himself?

The formality materialized the next day: A printed form on which filled-in blanks officially advised Mr. Curtis Charles Flood that his contract had been assigned to the Philadelphia Club of the National League. Signed by Vaughn P. Devine. Bing's personal bye-bye.

I was an expert on baseball's spurious paternalism. I was a connoisseur of its grossness. I had known that I was out of phase with management. I therefore had known that I might be traded. Yet now, when the industry was merely doing its thing, I took it personally. I felt unjustly cast out. Days passed before I began to see the problem whole.

Philadelphia. The nation's northernmost southern city. Scene of Richie Allen's ordeals. Home of a ball club rivaled only by the Pirates as the least cheerful organization in the league. When the proud Cardinals were riding a chartered jet, the Phils were still lumbering through the air in propeller jobs, arriving on the Coast too late to get proper rest before submitting to murder by the Giants and Dodgers. I did not want to succeed Richie Allen in the affections of that organization, its press and its catcalling, missile-hurling audience.

"I have only two choices," I told Marian, after treating her to another outburst of my inexhaustible anger and hurt. "I can go to Philadelphia or I can quit baseball altogether. I will not go to Philadelphia." The words of a typical baseball player, prostrated by the unchallengable rules of the industry.

I telephoned Bing Devine and told him that I would retire.

"That's entirely up to you, Curt. Good luck."

I told the reporters that I would retire. Nobody believed me. Traded players are forever threatening to pack it in. Few can afford to.

I wanted to cancel my Copenhagen trip, but Marian persuaded me to go. A change of scene would do me good.

She saw me off. We sat in the airport bar and she listened to me fume.

"I'm not going to let them do this to me," I announced. "They say that if I don't play in Philadelphia, I don't play at all. Right there, they shoot down my rights. They shoot me down as a man. I won't stand for it."

"Why not sue?" she asked.

I could have listed several reasons why not. The enormous cost, for one. The invulnerability of baseball, for another. The idea was impractical. I pushed it to the back of my mind. And there it grew.

Copenhagen was enchantment. If baseball was gone from my life, why not spend part of my time in Copenhagen? I wondered if I could open an American-style cocktail lounge, featuring the kind of rock musicians the Danes seldom heard except on records. I met Claire, a beautiful black Dane who spoke several languages fluently and knew the restaurant business. Yes, she would run such a place for me. Yes, she would help me find a location. Yes, she would be able to come to the States for a week or two and see how Americans operate. Her husband endorsed the idea. I would return home, try to put my baseball affairs in order, come back to Denmark. And, if all was still well, bring Claire to America for her instructional tour.

John Quinn, general manager of the Phillies, had been trying to reach me. He was in St. Louis on business.

"Mr. Quinn, you're wasting your time. I've made my decision."

"Can't you spare a few minutes for a chat?"

I met him at a hotel and was impressed. He was warm and understanding. He told me that the Philadelphia operation was being overhauled. Good new players were coming. A new ball park was in construction. Money was there for me. I agreed to see him again. I no longer was bothered about Philadelphia, as such. I was thinking more clearly. The problem was no particular city but was the reserve clause, which afflicted all players equally no matter where.

I dropped in on Allan H. Zerman, a young lawyer who counseled the operators of the photography business that bore my name. I liked him. He was the only man who had ever refused to take free World Series tickets from me. He had helped my brother Carl. I told him my story in fairly clear perspective. I no longer was bleeding. The issue was not me alone but the reserve system. Like thousands of players before me, I had been caught in its machinery. Before being ground to bits, I'd get out.

"St. Louis is my home," I said. "I'm known and liked here. I have business possibilities here. What the hell is there for me in Philadelphia? Screw 'em. I'm quitting."

"There's one other alternative," said Zerman.

"Are you talking about suing baseball?"

"Have you considered the idea?" he parried.

It had been germinating in me for weeks. Sooner or later, someone would challenge baseball's right to treat human beings like used cars. If this lawyer had not ruled out the possibility of a suit, why should I?

I telephoned Marvin Miller for an appointment and flew to New York to pick his brains.

"I want to sue baseball on constitutional grounds," I told him. His eyebrows rose. "I want to give the courts a chance to outlaw the reserve system. I want to go out like a man instead of disappearing like a bottle cap."

Marvin looked at me hard.

"How much thought have you given this?"

"Plenty. I should be able to negotiate for myself in an open market and see just how much money this little body is worth. I shouldn't be confronted with an either-or propo-

sition like the one now facing me. Somebody needs to go
up against the system. I'm ready."

"A lawsuit might take two or three years," said Marvin.
"It would cost a fortune. And you could lose, you know.
Others have."

"I could also win."

Marvin wouldn't let me off the hook.

"If you have any idea about becoming the first black
manager, you can forget it after suing. You can also forget
jobs as a coach or scout."

"I never had a chance anyway."

"Your present salary is around ninety thousand, right?
You're only thirty-one. Think of the money you'd lose by
staying out of the game during the next two or three seasons."

"You're not telling me anything I don't know."

"Is there anything in your personal life that they could
smear you with? They would."

"You haven't begun to scare me yet. Let's sue."

He took a deep breath.

"Not yet, please," he insisted. "I won't raise a finger to
help you until I'm sure that you've given enough thought
to all the possibilities. Go back to St. Louis and think.
When you're done thinking, start all over again. Don't
commit yourself to this until you have covered every detail
and are sure that the positive outweighs the negative.
Please."

I promised.

While in New York, I spent four hours over drinks and
dinner with John Quinn. A lady at an adjoining table
leaned over and said, "I know you from somewhere. Don't
tell me. Lou Brock!"

In situations like that, you get up and introduce yourself
before they have a chance to call you Jackie Robinson,

Satchel Paige and every other black ball player they can name. We all look alike.

"I'm Curt Flood," I said, "and this is John Quinn, general manager of the Phillies. I'm with them now."

Technically, it was true. In my haste to appease and silence the woman, I had omitted the details. The flat assertion may have signified more to Quinn than it did to me. It may have accounted for his perplexity when I filed suit. He had thought that I looked upon myself as a Phillie. He blamed Marvin Miller for changing my mind. This was untrue, and as unfair to Marvin as to me.

That evening, Quinn offered me a combination of salary and reimbursement for spring training expenses that would have raised my 1970 earnings above $100,000. When somebody talks that kind of money one does not respond with a flat no. Marvin Miller had advised me to think. Quinn's proposition would give me more to think about.

"How can you pay me all that expense money?" I asked.

"Don't worry about it. Let us handle it."

I told him that I would let him know.

I holed up in my St. Louis apartment and followed Marvin's instructions. The more deeply I explored myself, the more determined I became to take baseball to court. I was in luck. Until me, no player had been able to do himself the honor of committing so fundamental an act in behalf of his profession. Danny Gardella, a Giant outfielder blacklisted for playing in the Mexican League, had sued the owners and had won in the Circuit Court of Appeals. But he had been persuaded to settle for cash.

I would not settle out of court for any amount, unless the bargain included employer-employee relations of a kind acceptable to me and the Major League Baseball Players Association. I had little money, but I was fortified by what I am not ashamed to call spiritual resources. I had spent

good years with Johnny Jorgensen. I would do us both
proud by trying to improve my own corner of society before
moving on. Win or lose, the baseball industry would never
be the same. I would leave my mark.

"Marvin, I'm going ahead with it. Can you help?"
"It's possible. Come to our Executive Board meeting in
San Juan on December 13 and talk to the player reps."
I went. I spoke for at least half an hour. I told the players
that I was going to proceed with the suit whether I got
Association help or not, but that I needed all the backing
I could get. I explained my beliefs about the reserve system
and the unreasonable powers it gave to the club owners.
I spoke of the affronts to human dignity of a system that
indentured one man to another. I pointed out that fair
bargaining and real professionalism would remain distant
hopes in baseball unless I fought my fight.

The men questioned me closely. Many wanted to make
sure that I was not engaged in a classic ploy—threatening
suit in hope that the Phillies would raise the ante. Others
wondered how I would react if baseball offered to settle a
few hundred thousand dollars on me, out of court.

"I can't be bought," I said.

Tom Haller asked the good question, referred to much
earlier in these pages, about a possible link between my
suit and black militance. The discussion was thoughtful,
serious and heartening.

Nobody trotted out the threadbare and entirely insup-
portable argument—heard for so many years in so many
locker rooms—that modification of the reserve system
would ruin baseball. The Association had grown up.

The board excused me from the meeting and then voted
(25–0) to support my case. It authorized the Association
office to retain the best possible counsel for me.

Time was precious. Marvin Miller wasted none. He called Mr. Justice Arthur J. Goldberg, his former colleague in the steelworkers union, and asked him to consider taking my case. Mr. Goldberg already understood the basic issues, having been involved years before in a similar case that did not get to court. He invited me to meet him in his office.

Mr. Goldberg is a well-turned-out man with unmussed white hair and an unmussed mind. I was nervous about meeting him, partly because I was a stranger to conferences in the private offices of former Supreme Court justices, and partly because I sensed that my future might depend on the impression I made. He put me at ease by getting right to the facts, discussing the subject I knew best. Just as Marvin Miller had done, he played devil's advocate, reviewing all the dire possibilities to make sure that I had overlooked none.

"I just won't be treated as if I were an IBM card," I said.

"All right," he answered. "Let's go."

Ho-lee cow! Little old Curt Flood had him the most famous lawyer in the world.

On December 24, I fired the opening shot, a letter to Bowie Kuhn, the Commissioner of Baseball, with copies to John Quinn, Marvin Miller and the press. The letter said:

Dear Mr. Kuhn:

After twelve years in the major leagues, I do not feel that I am a piece of property to be bought and sold irrespective of my wishes. I believe that any system which produces that result violates my basic rights as a citizen and is inconsistent with the laws of the United States and of the several States.

It is my desire to play baseball in 1970, and I am capable of playing. I have received a contract offer from the Phila-

delphia club, but I believe I have the right to consider offers
from other clubs before making any decisions. I, therefore,
request that you make known to all Major League clubs my
feelings in this matter, and advise them of my availability
for the 1970 season.

The reporters swarmed. Was I going to sue? Was Arthur
Goldberg actually going to represent me? Did I really think
I could defeat baseball? Could baseball survive without
the reserve clause? I refused all comment, pending the
Commissioner's reply. It came under a December 30 date-
line, and started promisingly.

"I certainly agree with you," wrote Kuhn, "that you, as
a human being, are not a piece of property to be bought
and sold. That is fundamental to our society and I think
obvious. However," he veered, "I cannot see its applica-
bility to the situation at hand.

"You have entered into a current playing contract with
the St. Louis club, which has the same assignment provisions as those in your annual Major League contracts
since 1956. Your present contract has been assigned in
accordance with its provisions by the St. Louis club to the
Philadelphia club. . . ."

He also pointed out that the reserve system was em-
bodied in the basic agreements negotiated by the owners
and the Association. This was not true. The Association
has never agreed to the reserve system and has always questioned its legality. On the other hand, Kuhn did not mention that the owners had been refusing to negotiate changes
in the reserve system. In case I had doubted it before, I
now saw that we faced a long and punishing fight.

Mr. Goldberg's first step was to ask for an injunction
under the Sherman and Clayton Antitrust Laws, plus ap-
plicable state laws. The goal was to invalidate the trade,

make me a free agent and, most important, end the reserve system as a violation of the antitrust laws.

Robin Roberts told the press that "going to court is the wrong way." He still believed that some day sweet reason would persuade the owners to relent. Carl Yastrzemski complained that the Association's executive board should not have supported the suit. He demanded a referendum of all players. (The Association's collective bargaining proposals for revision of the reserve system had been drafted after a survey of the players.) Willie Mays allowed that he would not object to being traded, so long as the paychecks were large enough. Joe Cronin and Warren Giles warned about the ruination of the game and deplored my departure from the path of collective bargaining between the Association and the owners.

Eddie Kranepool described Yastrzemski as a yo-yo for the owners. Jackie Robinson, Bob Gibson, Dal Maxvill, Lou Brock, Rich Allen and dozens of others came flat out in behalf of the principle I was trying to advance.

Robinson said, "I think Curt is doing a service to all players in the leagues, especially for the younger players coming up who are not superstars. All he is asking for is the right to negotiate. It doesn't surprise me that he had the courage to do it. He's a very sensitive man concerned about the rights of everybody. We need men of integrity like Curt Flood and Bill Russell who are involved in the area of civil rights and who are not willing to sit back and let Mr. Charlie dictate their needs and wants for them. . . ."

A bit flattering in spots, but balm for my spirit.

Justice Goldberg informed me that during preliminary conferences, baseball's representatives rejected his attempts to avoid litigation. He had pointed out to the eminent Paul Porter that the problems could be arbitrated, or could be resolved by negotiation with the Players Association.

"Not practical," replied Porter.

Commissioner Bowie Kuhn was upset because I had made it plain that I would remain out of baseball while the issue was being contested. Goldberg told him at one conference that he had advised me that to play baseball while suing would hurt my case and might even cause its removal from the docket. Federal courts do not accept a case unless it is plainly a legitimate dispute. For me to play might make the whole issue hypothetical—what lawyers call "moot."

Kuhn reacted to this with great self-assurance, as though playing cat-and-mouse with the average witness. He was picking on the wrong man and should have known it.

Said Kuhn, "You mean, Mr. Justice, that *you* are advising Mr. Flood not to play?"

Goldberg jumped on him. "If you want to do any quoting," he said, "you had better be accurate in what you quote. The decision about whether Mr. Flood will play will be made by Mr. Flood. I have given him legal advice as to the impact of his decision. The decision is his. The only quotations you are authorized to make are (a) Mr. Flood will make the decision and (b) as to his reasons for not playing, he does not wish to be considered a piece of property and he considers the reserve rules both immoral and illegal. That is all you may quote."

Later, Kuhn asked with apparent dismay, "Is it true that negotiations are out—that the suit will proceed regardless?" Again Goldberg took him apart. "You have a terrible habit of misquoting," he said. "It is my understanding that if appropriate modifications can be made through negotiation, they would satisfy Curt Flood. Therefore, if you want to carry out your legal right to negotiate, please do so."

Comparatively few newspaper, radio and television journalists seemed able to understand what I was doing. That a

ball player would pass up a $100,000 year was unthinkable.
The player's contention that he was trying to serve a human
cause was somehow unbelievable. Who had ever heard of
anyone giving up $100,000 for a principle? For them, the
only plausible explanation was derangement. Or perhaps
I was a dupe of Marvin Miller. And, in any case, I would
surely show up in time for spring training. I wasn't that
crazy. As a matter of fact, more than one newsman nudged
my ribs with his elbow and winked conspiratorially about
the money he thought I might blackmail from the Phillies
with this suit. I began to wonder if the whole goddamned
country wasn't infected with moral corruption. Some of the
same people who criticized me for threatening the Good of
the Game made it clear enough that they would respect my
acumen if I abandoned the Players Association, disavowed
honor and signed for a higher salary than the Phillies had
previously offered.

For the record, and to be as fair as possible about the
press, the myopia was not universal. The syndicated col-
umnists Red Smith and Jim Murray knew what was afoot
and said so. Leonard Koppett reported the case and its
background with entire accuracy in *The New York Times,*
whose sports columnist, Robert Lipsyte, also understood.
Gene Ward of New York's *Daily News* and Howard Cosell
and Kyle Rote of television were others who seemed neither
confused, cynical nor enraged. *Sports Illustrated* and *Sport*
also presented the facts without hysteria. No doubt many
others played it straight. But I do not subscribe to a clipping
service, nor spend my life glued to the radio and television
sets. I can say with conviction that the preponderance of
material I read and heard was distressingly cynical and
ill-informed. Nothing I said in interviews got through to
such people. These guys evidently felt that responsibility
to principle was the hallucination of a nut.

Upset as I was by the zeal with which so many commentators were supporting the position of Bowie Kuhn, I was happy to take a telephone call from David Oliphant, a Connecticut businessman who wanted to talk to me about a book. It turned out that Dave himself had been harpooned by a phase of the reserve system neglected in these pages but immensely important. A phenomenal pitcher as a New York high school boy, he signed with the New York Yankees for a $3,000 bonus and spent two-and-a-half seasons shunting around the team's lesser farm clubs. The treatment he got was similar to mine during the two seasons with the Cincinnati Reds. Oliphant is Jewish. So they sent him to a club whose manager, a rabid anti-Semite, ostracized him—except when threatening to get rid of "that Jewboy." Concluding that the Yankees really did not want him, Dave asked for his release, hoping to connect with another organization.

After considerable haggling, the Yankees actually sold Dave's contract to his father for $2,000! Dave then caught on with the Dodgers, who were rich in pitching talent. He almost made the big club, but not quite. His record indicated that he could pitch for other major-league teams, but the terms of the reserve system condemned him to years in bushes, hoping that Don Newcombe or Carl Erskine or Don Drysdale or Preacher Roe might wear out. He finally left baseball. At one point, his anguished father made such a stink—and seemed so ready to expose the Yankees— that they refunded $1,000 of the money they had gouged from the Oliphants for the kid's release!

Dave loved baseball, just as most of the rest of us do. He loved to play the game. He loved the cameraderie. But he detested the industry's barbarism, its indifference to human dignity. For years, he had been waiting for a whack at the reserve system. He was thrilled at what I was doing.

He thought that I should write a book. I could tell my story without interruption or modification by anybody. I agreed. Dave introduced me to Herbert M. Alexander, publisher of Trident Press. Herb recommended the writer, Richard Carter.

Carter arrived in St. Louis at the end of February, while I was on pins and needles awaiting the decision on our plea for a Federal injunction. Judge Irving Ben Cooper, of the U.S. District Court for the Southern District of New York, had heard the legal arguments with great enjoyment. Instead of calling a brief recess, he beamed that it was time for "a seventh-inning stretch." At the end of the arguments, he said, "Now you have thrown the ball to me and I hope I don't muff it." I think I must have been the grimmest person in the courtroom. My sense of humor was on the injury list. I wanted the issues resolved quickly so that I could play baseball in 1970.

Nobody really believed that Judge Cooper would rule on the legality of the reserve system. Every precedent indicated that this was a job for the U.S. Supreme Court. Nevertheless, it was theoretically possible that he might liberate me to play ball while the broader issues were being tried. He declared that the law forbade it. On March 4, 1970, when my body was aching for the exertions of baseball, he denied the injunction and recommended that the merits of the reserve system be dealt with in a full-dress trial.

The press descended. Marian was ready with a prepared statement from me. "The failure to obtain a restraining order means that I have lost my one chance to play ball this year. I can only hope that after a full hearing on the merits that my position will have been vindicated and that my career will not have been ended by the time lost in pursuing what I believe to be right."

It was not enough. The networks and newspapers demanded interviews. I told Marian to stall them for a while.

"I don't want to see those guys," I told Carter. "I don't want to see them and put on a brave front. I don't want to tell them that the money is inconsequential to me because I can paint and get rich in private enterprise and do anything I want. It's a lot of bullshit. I'm a baseball player and I'm supposed to play out my string. I'm supposed to be in Florida now, romping around and hitting the ball and cussing with Gibson and banging the chicks."

I had never ducked reality, yet had never confronted it in such quantity, and had never enjoyed it less. I had declared myself ready to make sacrifices for a principle, and now I was getting the bill. Baseball, the thing I did best in this world, was finished. Very likely, I was through. The photography business, in which I had had such hope, was foundering. I had not been able to pick up a paintbrush in weeks. The Copenhagen venture was in its death throes, sex having caused complications which neither Claire nor I could handle.

"All right," I said to Marian. "Set up a press conference for tomorrow afternoon. If I can't stand the heat, I'm supposed to get out of the kitchen. I don't know whether I can take it, but I'm staying in the goddamned kitchen."

At noon, I took Claire to the airport for what both of us knew was a last good-bye. I primed my pump at the airport bar and then proceeded to Allan Zerman's office, every room of which was filled with television equipment, tape recorders and interrogators. I had my largest and darkest glasses on, hoping that nobody could see the despair in my face.

I went through my usual spiel. Nothing had changed, I said. I would proceed step by step until a conclusion was reached. I assumed that our next move would be a trial, but I had not yet consulted Mr. Justice Goldberg. Yes, I supposed that my career was over, although I was ready to resume at any time possible. No, I was not trying to ruin the national pastime. Yes, a principle was worth more than $100,000 a year. Yes, a peon remains a peon no matter how much money you give him. It reminded me of who I was and what I was about. I could scarcely walk when I left the place, yet I felt better. I had been upchucking for two days, but now it stopped.

The strain got to Marian. She came down with a nasal hemorrhage in the middle of the night. Nothing we did stopped the bleeding. At the hospital she caused consternation by insisting that her next of kin was Curt Flood. After winning that battle, she submitted to treatment. She had lost a great deal of blood. But we had caught it in time. I cried for her and for myself and for the road we had come together. She stayed in bed for a couple of days on doctor's orders and then, defiantly, resumed charge of me.

"Get to bed, Babe, for God's sake," I commanded.

"I'm too busy."

"Get to bed."

"What are you going to do about Jim Lefebvre? He called again about the portraits of his family. He's such a nice man."

"Jim Lefebvre, Jim Lefebvre. That's all I hear from you! I'm tired of this constant talk about men! It's sick, I tell you! Sick!"

The banter had returned to normal.

Dave Oliphant came to St. Louis to see how the book was going. He conceded that Judge Cooper's decision and other events beyond our control might well have deflected Dick Carter and me from our work. He commended to our attention that vodka was not the best fuel for the kind of vehicle we were trying to assemble. He dragged me outside for a game of catch. It was just the right therapy. First catch of the 1970 season. I was as limber as ever. My arm felt great.

"I could be ready to play in a couple of weeks," I said.

"Keep your chin up," said Dave. "They're going to settle this thing out of court. Wait and see."

The trial was to be held in New York before Judge Cooper. Shortly before it started, Monte Irvin telephoned. Monte had been a great player in the old Negro leagues. In 1949, at the age of thirty, he had come up with the Giants and starred for them. And now he was working in the office of Commissioner Bowie Kuhn. He told Marian that the Commissioner wanted to have a chat with me. A private heart-to-heart. She said that she would relay the message.

Two days later Monte telephoned again and got me. The Commissioner had cleared the whole thing with Justice Goldberg's office. Would I meet him in Los Angeles? For a strictly informal chat?

"Damnit, Monte, the last guy who saw the Commissioner for an informal chat wound up getting a boot in the ass." I was thinking of Denny McLain.

"He'd have been in worse trouble if he hadn't come in," said Monte. This sounded to me like a threat.

Then came a third call from Monte. I was not at home.

"The Commissioner definitely wants to talk to Curt," he told Marian. "He's willing to pay Curt's expenses to Los Angeles."

"What on earth does he want to talk about?" she asked.

"The Commissioner has worked out a deal. Curt can play for any National League club of his choice without jeopardizing the litigation."

"Oh, come on, Monte!" laughed Marian. "You know very well that the Commissioner can't change the rules of

the Federal judiciary. If Curt plays ball, his case becomes
moot. Now tell me what the Commissioner really wants."

"He's a very compassionate man," said Monte. "He
wants everybody to be happy."

"Oh?" said Marian.

"This is the last door open," threatened Monte. "If I
don't hear from you by tomorrow, I'll know that you've
closed the door."

"Thank you, Monte."

A few days later, I got a telegram from Bowie Kuhn:

> AM DISAPPOINTED YOU DECLINED MY INVITATION FOR A PER-
> SONAL CONFERENCE IN LOS ANGELES ON FRIDAY. I DESIRED AN
> OPPORTUNITY TO DISCUSS WITH YOU PERSONALLY YOUR BASE-
> BALL CAREER WITHOUT PREJUDICE TO THE BASIC ISSUES
> INVOLVED IN THE PENDING LITIGATION. MY COUNSEL HAS AS-
> CERTAINED FROM YOUR COUNSEL THAT THE LATTER HAD NO
> OBJECTIONS TO SUCH A CONFERENCE WITH THE EXPLICIT CON-
> DITION THAT HE WAS NOT RECOMMENDING THAT YOU ASSENT
> OR DECLINE. THIS IS TO ADVISE YOU THAT IF YOU RECONSIDER I
> WILL CONTINUE TO BE AVAILABLE.

I now knew that someday the owners of baseball would
instruct Kuhn to issue a similar invitation to Marvin Miller
and the leadership of the Major League Baseball Players
Association and me, to discuss revisions in the reserve
clause. Life was brightening.

But the trial was dull. The points at issue were matters of
constitutional and legal scholarship. Testimony was less
significant than the arguments contained in the briefs. So
we got a parade of testimonials from witnesses who opined
that the reserve system was bad or unnecessary or both,
after which the defense produced testimonials from witnesses who contended that the system was vital to the
perpetuation of the game. The proceedings held little

interest for me after I caught their drift. One high spot was the arrival in court of Jackie Robinson, who came directly to me, shook my hand and congratulated me on my stand. His praise choked me up. The defense provided a certain sad amusement by its repeated assertion that modification of the reserve rules would ruin "baseball as we know it."

What they meant was that the change might reduce their profits. The term "baseball as we know it" denoted a national pastime immutable in form, because any change might displease or confuse the beloved fan. I was deeply grateful and rousingly entertained when Leonard Koppett wrote on June 14, 1970 in *The New York Times*:

As for 'baseball as we know it'—as who knows it? And when?

Is baseball as 'we' know it sixteen teams playing 154-game schedules, twenty teams playing 162-game schedules, or twenty-four teams playing in four divisions with playoffs to decide pennant winners?

Is it independent minor-league teams and free competition for new players, or subsidized minors with a free-agent draft?

Is it unlimited control of hundreds of players by any one farm system, or an 'unrestricted draft' that limits certain control to the forty-man roster?

Is it a half-century of immovable franchises crammed into eleven cities in the northeast quadrant of the country, or sixteen changes in the major-league map in the last seventeen years?

Is it a game played on natural grass or on a synthetic surface? Is it one in which starting pitchers complete 75 percent of the game or 25 percent? Is it a game where men who hit .400 fail to win a batting title or one in which a man with .301 does? Is it a lively ball or a dead ball, symmetrical stadia

or old ball parks, big gloves or little gloves, 400 major-league
players or 600 major-league players, with a legal spitball or
without, with two umpires on the field or four, under lights
or all in the daytime?

The reserve clause has been 100 percent effective since
1915, when the Federal League folded. All the above changes
have come about since then. The only aspect 'preserved' by
the reserve system is the reserve system itself.

Frederick Douglass was a Maryland slave who taught
himself to read. "If there is no struggle," he once said,
"there is no progress. Those who profess to favor freedom,
and yet deprecate agitation, are men who want crops without plowing up the ground. . . . Power concedes nothing
without a demand. It never did and never will."

To see the Curt Flood case in that light is to see its entire
meaning. I have asked the Federal courts to affirm that
national policy requires reasonably equitable relations between employers and employees, and that baseball is no
exception. I have promised to pursue the matter to the
Supreme Court of the United States, if necessary. I have
no choice. The owners left me none. Their refusal to stop
violating the antitrust laws meant that I could obtain my
rights only through litigation. After the courts rule that
the present reserve system is unlawful, the employers will
be obligated to do what they should have done years ago.
They will sit down with the players and negotiate reasonable conditions of employment.

13

The Senator from Copenhagen

I spent most of the summer of 1970 bedding and boozing and waiting for Judge Irving Ben Cooper to shunt my case toward the U.S. Supreme Court where it belonged. Apart from the lawsuit and occasional sessions with Larry Albert of The Aunts and Uncles, I was involved in nothing useful. I lacked the patience to paint. I refused employment in the photography businesses that used my name. Illogically—even superstitiously—I avoided gainful pursuits, as if they might indicate that I was trying to start a new career in expectation of losing my case. So I marked time. And I slowly went to seed.

In August, Marian managed to get my concentrated attention for the first time in weeks. I found myself focusing on some unpleasant truths.

"The Curt Flood corporations are on the rocks," she was saying. "They're about to go under. You simply cannot go on like this."

"Don't curdle my vodka. It's a great big beautiful world. Love conquers all."

"Things are past the joking stage, dear. Try to listen to me."

"I'm as clear as a bell. The Curt Flood corporations are in deep trouble. Maybe I should put some money into them."

"Dear, you don't have enough and none is coming in. At the rate you're going, you'll be lucky to get through the year."

I had been whistling in the dark. I actually had believed that the businesses would keep me alive if the need arose. Their prosperity had been what I had in mind when I assured everyone that my commercial interests meant that suing posed no financial hardship for me. Failure of the corporations would be a crushing embarrassment.

"I'll be ashamed to show my goddamned face in St. Louis after playing bigshot all this time," I grieved. "I might as well clear out now, before the stuff hits the fan. I'm through in St. Louis baseball and I'm through in the town itself. Time to go, baby."

Marian looked stricken.

"I'll go to Copenhagen," I announced. "Nobody knows me. I can stretch a dollar further there. Maybe I can find a bar or restaurant to buy into. Best of all, I can sweat out the federal courts without having to worry about my image all the time. It will be a real vacation."

Marian finally agreed. I suppose she was in favor of anything that might stir me out of my vegetative stupor. I wondered whether she also felt, as I did, that my departure would be her liberation. She could now go back to Oakland and lead a genteel existence instead of cleaning up after me. I had been exploiting her terribly.

Brief inquiry confirmed that the businesses were indeed

on their way to hell, and that I could do nothing to salvage them. I packed my bags. Marian and I agreed that this was not a permanent good-bye. Just another bump in the road, this. I then flew away. She disposed of the apartment and drove to the Coast.

I found a pleasant room overlooking a yacht basin near Copenhagen. I bought a sketch pad and beret and grew a goatee. I played artist on street corners and in the happy hunting grounds known as Tivoli Gardens. "Little do these beautiful Danish pastries realize," I mused, "that the aesthetic black in the beret and goatee is actually Curt Flood, the famous St. Louis business tycoon and athlete, vacationing between triumphs."

I began negotiating to buy a restaurant, after finding someone able to help me run a business of that kind. I learned by mail that Judge Cooper had ruled, as expected, that the issues in my case could not be resolved at his level. American servicemen on leave from Germany told me that Bob Gibson was having a great year although the Cardinals were terrible. And then I discovered that my supposed vacation was not at all what I had planned.

Technically, but entirely without design, I was on the lam. The collapse of the photography businesses had hurt some people badly. They had struck back. A lawsuit or two was being filed against me. It was conceivable that neither the corporate nature of the businesses nor my own abstention from their affairs would free me of all legal responsibility.

All of a sudden, Copenhagen was no longer a vacation resort but a jail. To run away from social discomfort—as I surely had—was no worse than self-indulgent and silly. But to find that my flight had rescued me from more serious embarrassment was downright awful. Was the black champion of players' rights supposed to end like this—hiding from creditors in a Danish hotel room? And what a splendid combination of lawsuits to be involved in! One case majestically on its way to the Supreme Court and history. The others before some lowly tribunal concerned with unpaid bills.

While awaiting the arrival of more details, so that I'd know how best to proceed, I got a telephone call from a reporter on the *Washington Post*.

"What do you think of the deal?" he began.

"Deal?"

"Don't you know that the Washington Senators have acquired the rights to negotiate with you?"

It seemed that Robert E. Short, owner of the Washington club, had agreed to give Philadelphia a player just for the right to talk to me. A few minutes later, while I was pondering this strange development, Short telephoned.

"What's the possibility of us getting together?" he inquired, as if he were downstairs in the lobby instead of an ocean away.

"You know how I feel about the reserve clause, Mr. Short. And you know that the whole thing is in court. You know that I must talk to people in New York before I can even consider talking to you."

"Curt, you've already made your point in court. You've stayed out for a whole year. The rest is up to the Circuit Court of Appeals or the Supreme Court itself. You've got nothing more to gain by staying out of baseball."

"Maybe so, maybe not. The last I heard, I could not play without harming our case. If anything has changed, I'd love to know it."

"Come to New York as my guest," urged Short. "Talk to your lawyers. Then let's get together. I'm sure we can work something out that won't hurt your case but will put a lot of money into your pocket and help my ball club."

It all sounded unrealistic to me, but I could not resist a free trip to New York. I cabled Marvin Miller and took off. At worst, I'd learn at closer hand about the present status of the lawsuit. And about the real situation in St. Louis. God, I wanted to play baseball again. Could it possibly happen?

As usual, Marvin Miller addressed me with supreme objectivity. Just as he had not influenced me to file suit, he now refused to tell me whether or not to negotiate with Bob Short. It was entirely up to me.

"But would my playing in 1971 hurt our chances in the higher courts? Can a case be dismissed as moot *after* it has been tried and has entered the appeals process? Might not our situation be different now that the actual trial is over with?"

"That's a question for Arthur Goldberg," replied Marvin.

It was late October. Goldberg was in the thick of his campaign as Democratic candidate for governor of New York. Yet he took time to meet with Marvin, Dick Moss and me. He knew about my business reverses. He told me what I wanted to hear:

"By remaining out of baseball and giving up more than a hundred thousand dollars in income last season, you suffered real damages which go to the heart of your dispute with the reserve system. I therefore think that you could play in 1971 without hurting the case in the higher courts."

When he, Miller, Moss, Max Gitter (a Goldberg associate), and I met with Bob Short, we handed him a list of written proposals. In effect, these suggested that he give me a contract from which the key provisions of the reserve clause were eliminated. We asked him to agree (a) not to trade me without my consent, (b) to pay me the full year's salary even if I were cut from the team before the end of the season, and (c) to release me unconditionally if he and

I were unable to agree on terms for a 1972 renewal of the contract. We also demanded agreement that the owners would not argue in court that my presence on the playing field invalidated my suit.

Bob Short has been around. He is a lawyer and a trucking and hotel magnate who developed the almost bankrupt Los Angeles Lakers basketball franchise into a multi-million-dollar bonanza. He reviewed our demands without turning a hair. He agreed to them all. Goldberg and Gitter returned to their offices to draw up a memorandum embodying this agreement. Short and I were about to sign the first equitable player's contract in the history of major-league baseball! The precedent would be tremendously important—the first huge step toward industry-wide modification of the reserve system.

Three hours later, we reconvened. Short is usually a bluff, outgoing man but he was now curiously subdued. He explained that he was obliged to offer some second thoughts. For example, he no longer could agree to modify the standard reserve provisions in my contract.

"Commissioner Kuhn will not permit it," he said, sheepishly.

This meant that Short's fellow owners—his colleagues in the payment of Kuhn's salary and in the establishment of Kuhn's policy—had issued orders to restrain Bob Short.

Short had been given the word in a telephone conversation with Alexander (Sandy) Hadden, former counsel to the American League and now counsel to Kuhn. Hadden was still on the line. Shore consulted him frequently while talking to us. The owner of the Senators was empowered to agree that the contract could contain a covenant in which both parties stipulated that my playing was not prejudicial to the issues under dispute in court. And, if I insisted, the contract also could grant me veto power over one kind of trade.

"If you want, I can agree not to trade you to Philadelphia without your consent," he said.

By then we were all so shocked and angered by Short's retreat that we did not even laugh at the Philadelphia ploy. We simply rejected it.

And there we sat. The decision was up to me. I said that I needed time to think.

Short was in a hurry. He said that he would pay me "around a hundred thousand" for the season. Justice Goldberg suggested $110,000. Short grabbed it.

He then promised to help me straighten out my financial affairs. He also spoke of giving me a job during the off season. And, finally, he indicated he would not let the other owners force him to renege on his word to me.

"I made good-faith assurances," he said, "and I'll keep them."

This was better. But was it good enough?

I returned to my room and took stock. On the positive side:

1. Nobody—including myself—could justly accuse me of selling out my principles for money. I was not dropping my case against the owners. I would continue to pursue it until a resolution was reached either by court order or through negotiation with the Major League Baseball Players Association.

2. Apparently my playing would not prejudice higher courts against our appeal. I had Justice Goldberg's assurances on that score, and would get the owners' promise in writing not to try to defeat our suit on grounds that my playing undermined my arguments.

3. The $110,000 salary would help me get back on an even keel.

4. Short had offered me a job in the Florida Instructional League beginning in November. I could get into decent shape before spring training began. I could expect every opportunity to re-establish myself as a first-rate outfielder.

On the other hand:

1. Many fans would surely suppose that I had sold out or, at the very least, had been pressured into abandoning the fight. In 1970 I had called myself a $90,000-a-year slave and now I would be playing quietly for $110,000. This would tend to reaffirm public belief in the invincible power of the baseball establishment. Worse, it would encourage cynicism about the durability of principles—not only mine but everyone else's.

2. Many baseball players would be bitterly disappointed. Some might be hostile. They would wonder if I had used the Major League Baseball Players Association for the sole purpose of getting myself a $20,000 raise. That the Association had been supporting not Curt Flood himself but a suit against the hated reserve system would take much explaining. Months or years might pass, furthermore, until anyone could be absolutely certain that my return to uniform had not weakened our position. Meanwhile, I could expect a rough time. I would be baited as the self-styled man of principle who ran out of principle in one season. I would be ripped as the successful businessman who kept saying that "some things are more important than money" until his businesses disappeared and he signed with Washington. For money.

Too bad. Too bad for me. Too bad for those who might misunderstand or misrepresent me. Too bad that I had sacrificed only $100,000 or so in salary and only one year of my waning athletic career. I would have preferred enough wealth to pass up $100,000 a year for as long as it took the courts to rule on our principle. I would have preferred such wealth not only for its own green sake but because my public position would then have been uncomplicated. Too bad.

And too bad that I now was only a hop and a skip from bankruptcy. I called Marvin Miller and Dick Moss and Arthur Goldberg and told them that I would sign. I then called Short and signed. I went to Copenhagen for my clothes, and to explain why the restaurant deal would have to wait until the fall of 1971.

I then returned to the United States to get ready to do my thing.

Appendixes

APPENDIX A

Discussion with Commissioner Bowie K. Kuhn
at Major-League Baseball Players Association
Executive Board Meeting, December 14,
1969, San Juan, Puerto Rico.

[Note: The following is not an official transcript. It is an accurate reproduction of complete notes taken at the meeting.]

COMMISSIONER KUHN: I am sorry you chose to hold your meeting apart from the winter baseball meetings. I like to see all the important elements of baseball meeting in the same place at the same time. In the past two winters it was not especially constructive that your meetings were held at the same place as ours, but psychologically we are much more likely to pull together on things if we are all in the same vicinity. . . . Also, the baseball writers have asked me to convey their interest in all the meetings being held together. It is not helpful to meet in a place like Puerto Rico, where there is a press vacuum. Next year, we have tentatively decided that the winter meetings will be held in Tucson, subject to obtaining appropriate facilities.

With regard to the method of selecting the All-Star teams, I feel it should be changed. There is promotional value in fan participation. I am pressing ahead with my efforts to find a method for the fans to elect the teams and avoid the old Cincinnati problem of stacking the team with all the players from one club.

As to protective helmets with ear flaps, I feel strongly on this subject. It is a very important protective device. I understand the objections of players regarding hearing and vision. Recently, I've had meetings with a number of helmet manufacturers and Little League officials. They all claim that the problem is one of habit. Also, I've gone to a material-testing outfit to establish whether the present helmet with ear flaps is the best one or whether another should be designed. I'm going ahead with this and I ask that you all encourage your teammates to use it. It would be best if you set the example.

I sent to Marvin [Miller] a copy of the report of the Major League Planning Committee. The report faces some difficulties and has had some criticism, but I am convinced it is good and I am pursuing it. In essence, the report is designed to increase the legal powers of the office of the Commissioner, so that all involved can work more effectively together, especially with regard to the legislative aspects of baseball. Also, there is a psychological effect in putting everything together in one building. It would eliminate different interpretations of rules as between the two leagues.

With regard to the current bargaining, I won't talk of specifics. I note that I am more than a little involved. But in a general way, during the last year baseball has made some significant strides. This has come about for a number of reasons. I think I have made some contribution to that. Baseball has gotten into some trouble because of divisiveness, and not just between the two leagues. Our number-one position has just been jeopardized, not just because of the progress of football, but also by our own conduct and the real economic force of enormous competition in the field of entertainment. There are now all kinds of out-of-door recreation.

To the extent that we play baseball in the season and bargain to crises in the off-season, we are obviously imperiling baseball in areas in which we must compete. I've taken myself out of the bargaining and I can look at the problem more dispassionately than anyone else in baseball. You must find a new method. The application of reason and good will is all I can think of.

I recognize that this is hard to do where there are financial stakes. But unless we do it, the industry will be—and has been —seriously hurt. You should get what is fairly yours, but you must apply reason and good will in determining what is fairly yours. I have no answers, but you—the players and the clubs— are going to have to work out problems yourselves. I hope you have the good judgment to do so properly.

I think it important that I attend all your meetings in the future, even if I have nothing to say. It is important that I be available to the players.

MARVIN MILLER: I know you agree that it is important to speak frankly. That is the only way to communicate, which is what I shall try to do.

First, with regard to the location of this meeting, I don't quite understand your point. The fact is that two years ago we met in Mexico City during the winter baseball meetings and it was not very pleasant for anyone. I'm not saying who was at fault. Last year in San Francisco, we had almost a repeat performance. There was small contact with the owners, and we know there was some adverse feeling about our holding a press conference. It begins to look like, if we meet in the same city, that's not good, and if we meet in a different city, that's not good either. If we have a press conference that's not good, and if we meet in a place where there is a press vacuum, it's still not good.

We're not looking to please or displease the owners. The Players Association is an independent organization. But our experience of the last two years has not been in anyone's interest. More basically, however, if the owners have a business meeting, that is their business. We recognize that the owners are indeed kept busy during the winter meetings. We are not asked about the location of and the agenda for those meetings —and I'm not saying that we should be—but that is consistent with a joint convention approach. It doesn't make any sense.

With regard to the current bargaining, we are also concerned about the fact that we can't seem to resolve problems without going down to the wire. As you say, solutions are not easy. But we've tried to push for early negotiations, and every attempt we have made has been met with a cold reception. We have no solution to the problem. We do disagree, however, that baseball has been damaged by the problem. Last spring there were dire predictions by you and others that terrible things would happen to baseball because of the publicity attendant to our dispute at that time. Nothing happened like that. Baseball was not hurt. I don't mean to suggest that it was good for baseball, but it is a fact that baseball did not suffer.

As to the selection of All-Star teams, last July at your request this Board considered the matter and reported back to you that the players preferred the present system because they felt strongly that their performance could best and most fairly be judged by their peers. Notwithstanding that opinion, which you solicited, apparently you have decided that the fans will do the balloting.

Also at your request last July, the Board considered the question of the mandatory wearing of ear flaps. As we reported at that time, many players do have problems with the present design because of interference with vision and hearing. We did suggest, however, that a number of different designs be developed and that during spring training the players be given an opportunity to try them on an experimental basis, to see if any can overcome the problem inherent in the present design. If I understood what you said on this subject today, apparently you are consulting with everyone except players. All we can do is renew our suggestion and tell you that we would be happy to cooperate in an experiment to find the best design. If the players' views are not considered important, however, then that is quite another matter.

Finally, concerning your desire to attend all our meetings, even if you have nothing to say, we will be glad to put it to the Board. It is a highly unusual request. Frankly, if you have nothing to say, I don't think you should be here almost as a member of the Board. It is important when you do have something to talk about that you receive an opportunity to appear.

TOM HALLER: Mr. Kuhn, you talked about the importance of public opinion. I'm sure you're familiar with our poll of sportswriters concerning the length of the season, and that over ninety-five percent said it was too long. When you refuse to shorten the season, isn't public opinion being ignored? Isn't that inconsistent with your overall view?

KUHN: Sometimes we must go against public opinion when public opinion is not wise. We cannot do that regularly, however.

MIKE MCCORMICK: I want to ask about the situation in Cincinnati for the next year, where, as I understand, there will be Astroturf covering the complete field. Isn't this really bowing to football? Shouldn't we at least have a skin infield?

KUHN: The Cincinnati thing is an experiment. It is partially to accommodate football. But the infield will be painted brown. Football must paint it out. If we use this surface universally, we will have fewer rainouts, and that is good. Also, where this turf is used, many believe that players will be less susceptible to injuries. And we will get a more regularized game with truer bounces and faster ground balls. We fail to experiment at our peril where there are pros and cons.

MCCORMICK: I think it's a mistake to eliminate grass. It's even worse to eliminate dirt. That's how my players feel.

KUHN: Not always will baseball come into a stadium as a prime tenant. Where we are an equal tenant with football, we run into problems of overlapping. With artificial turf, the chances of tearing up the field are decreased.

JIM BUNNING: But that's changing the game. It's not the same game on a field completely covered with Astroturf.

KUHN: I agree the game is bound to be changed. But that shouldn't be a factor unless it is clearly an adverse change.

BROOKS ROBINSON: I heard that the players in Portland last year, where there was complete Astroturf covering, didn't care for the situation.

KUHN: I talked to some of the players and they said it was perfectly acceptable, except when it was wet there was a danger of oversliding on the base paths. They tried spreading some kind of granules on the base paths, but when they got wet the same problem existed.

ED KRANEPOOL: What kind of shoes did they wear?

KUHN: The Reds say players will wear regular spikes.

BOB LOCKER: I've heard the view that it's good for baseball if the parks are different, and I agree. It is an important part of the game. If every ball takes the same hop every time, it takes some suspense out of the game.

KUHN: Many people in club operations agree with you. But we cannot put our heads in the sand and avoid the Cincinnati experiment. Different outfield dimensions are important too, in my opinion.

RON BRAND: At Houston, we found there was a problem of starting and stopping on Astroturf. It is a problem that affects players' careers. Many players seemed to develop leg problems as a result of running on the artificial turf. Dirt was the only saving grace. Has this been considered?

KUHN: Yes. Some people think that legs take less pounding because of the padding. Therefore, there is a difference of view.

DENNY LEMASTER: Legs, knees and shins bother us. We look forward to going on the road to run on grass.

ROBINSON: That is what I have been told, not only by baseball players but football players, too.

BUNNING: The problem is made worse because of the differences between parks and the need to play on entirely different playing surfaces.

STEVE HAMILTON: That is especially true with a crowded, two-game schedule.

MCCORMICK: The only good things I have heard have been in a football context. Therefore, it seems to me it is a clear concession to football.

KUHN: The problems must be evaluated. Therefore, I have reactivated the study committee on Astroturf. Its purpose will be to develop standards. Some people said that I should come out against the Cincinnati experiment. I didn't do that, because we must experiment.

PHIL REGAN: Have players been consulted?

KUHN: The committee is Bing Devine, Clark Griffith, Bob Howsam and one other. I believe they have talked to players.

MAX ALVIS: I'm recovering from a knee injury. I've never been on Astroturf before, and I'm concerned about reinjury. I suspect that I am especially vulnerable to the problems of Astroturf.

KUHN: The consensus is that it is not difficult to adapt to.

MOE DRABOWSKY: If we have injuries, will the experiment be discontinued?

KUHN: Under what was adopted, the Astroturf would be removed.

HAMILTON: The people on your committee are probably competent. But we have had no say about what clearly involves our careers. Our considerations have not been taken into account.

REGAN: You have talked about improving the image of baseball. What about the rule in Chicago against signing autographs before a game? I think that's bad for baseball.

MILLER: We mentioned this problem to the Commissioner before. There are different rules in the two leagues.

KUHN: Basically they are the same. But I agree with Phil Regan. I asked both leagues to consider modifications of those regulations so that, one, up to a certain time before a game, kids would be able to come down into the box seats for autographs, and two, ballplayers in uniform would be available to kids at designated spots. The leagues have agreed to number two, but not to number one.

REGAN: Can you tell us why there are no owners at our negotiating meetings?

KUHN: I can't tell you why. I do think that Chub Feeney, now that he has become National League President, will be an asset.

MILLER: The players are concerned about the report of playoff expenses which were deducted from the players' pool. There are enormous differences between the individual club expenses, and some of the expense items appear very clearly improper under the rule. What is particularly disturbing is that the bills were apparently paid from your office without questions and examination. Can you enlighten us?

KUHN: I cannot. I am aware that there are marked differences between the clubs. The bills were reviewed by Charles Segar with the two league attorneys.

KRANEPOOL: We notice that the players were charged with the cost of constructing television booths, even though they did not share in the television revenue from the playoffs.

KUHN: You should discuss that with Mr. Gaherin and his group.

MCCORMICK: There is a great deal of concern by the players regarding the problem of establishing a good-faith relationship between our Association and the owners. I hope you understand that. It will take great strength on your side and on our side.

KUHN: The people on the other side feel the same way about you.

LOCKER: Your side and our side must both be interested in good-faith negotiations. We are, but your Player Relations Committee seems to be mainly interested in delay. If you want to, we can make an agreement early.

MILLER: Bob makes a very good point. There is no reason why negotiations should be delayed and should drag on to the point where they must be resolved in a crisis atmosphere. There seems to be a fear on the part of your people of offering reasonable solutions too early. The only way that fear can be dispelled is if you try us. That is the only way a mature relationship can develop. We can recognize a reasonable proposal when we see one, and we could have the basis for an agreement now. Don't say to us over a period of months, "No, no, no, we'll offer fifty cents a year." That's not constructive.

KUHN: I just wanted to mention one other thing. As you know, I recently traveled to Vietnam. It was the greatest experience I ever had in my life. I hope you will participate in these tours if you are asked, and I hope you will urge the players on your teams to do likewise. It is really something.

APPENDIX B

Statement by August A. Busch, Jr., President,
St. Louis Cardinals, to Cardinal players at a meeting
attended by the working press and members of the
boards of Anheuser-Busch, Inc., and the baseball club
on March 22, 1969, at St. Petersburg, Florida.

[Author's note: What follows is the full text of the statement. Its grammar, punctuation and paragraphing are faithfully transcribed from a pamphlet published by the directors of Anheuser-Busch and the Cardinals and circulated to stockholders. In a foreword to the pamphlet, the directors remark that "the philosophy he expressed has even wider significance and application than to baseball players alone. . . ." I agree.]

Gentlemen:

I'd like you all to know that before I came here today, I talked over what I wanted to say with Dick Meyer, our Executive Vice President; Bing Devine, our General Manager; Stan Musial, our Senior Vice President; and Red Schoendienst, our Manager.

As you know, Bing, Stan and Red have devoted all their lives to baseball . . . and Dick Meyer has been Executive Vice President of the Cardinals ever since our company, Anheuser-Busch, bought the club.

Some of the things that concern me deal with our team specifically and with baseball generally.

After talking to my staff, I decided to discuss my views with you all and get them off my chest. That's what I'm doing now.

This meeting may be regarded by some as an unusual pro-

cedure. But, since I regard the situation in baseball as unusual
. . . and critical . . . I don't know any better way to communicate with you than to talk to you face to face as I'm doing now.

You'll notice that I'm speaking from notes. That's chiefly
because I don't want my remarks to be misunderstood.

Let me begin by reminding you that it is just seventeen years
ago this month that our company, Anheuser-Busch, bought
the Cardinals. Our first concern was to keep the Cardinals in
St. Louis when a change in the ownership of the club was being
forced.

Most of you know what we have done since then . . . not
only to keep the team in St. Louis, but also to try to build the
best ball club possible . . . and we have spent millions of dollars
doing just that.

I'm very happy to say that both our players and our fans have
responded magnificently.

Of course, over the years we have had some headaches, and
we have had some heartaches. We also have had many pleasant
moments.

Gentlemen, I don't think there is any secret about the fact
that I am not a very good loser. One thing is for sure . . . I don't
like to lose. I don't like to lose in baseball . . . and I don't like
to lose in the beer business.

For that reason, you can well understand that there have been
a number of times in the past seventeen years when I felt like
giving the club away.

On the whole, we have been very glad that we made the
decision we did to buy the Cardinals.

So far as I know, we were the first company of its kind to
own a major league team.

Some people, however, didn't agree with our decision to get
into baseball. In fact, a special bill was introduced in the Senate
of the United States, back in 1953, to legislate us out of baseball. There were committee hearings in the senate, and we were
forced to attend meetings to defend our right to own and to
operate this ball club.

But, that's water over the dam. Many of the things that hap-

pened since our entry into baseball have certainly gone far
beyond anything we dreamed of in 1953.

All we really set out to do seventeen years ago was to buy a
major league baseball team to keep it in St. Louis.

Never in our wildest dreams would we have believed that we
would end up buying an old ball park . . . spending several
million dollars more to make it clean and attractive for our
fans.

Certainly, we would never have imagined that we would be
investing five million dollars more in a new ball park that didn't
belong to us . . . and which would increase our rental costs by
about five hundred percent . . . in addition to giving up about
a half-million dollars annually in other revenue we realized from
our own property.

In fact, we gave up all sources of revenue, except gate receipts
and radio and television rights, to help make the new stadium
possible.

The last thing I want to do at this time is to go into a long
discussion about business.

But, since we have been through long and very highly publicized pension discussions . . . and since our salary and contract
discussions have made headlines all over . . . I believe it is
perfectly in order that you should know something about the
front office operations.

I believe you should know something about the decisions we
must make . . . the risks we must take . . . the problems we
face . . . and so on

Ball parks and all the things it takes to put a major league
team on the field don't just happen.

They do take a lot of planning and hard work by a lot of
people doing many different jobs.

You don't put over two million people into a stadium by
wishful thinking.

It takes hundreds of people, working every day, to make it
possible for eighteen men to play a game of baseball that lasts
for about two hours.

I don't think we should lose sight of that fact.

I don't believe it is out of place either to remind you of the large number of civic-minded businessmen and unions in our community . . . who put up over twenty million dollars of their money . . . and then put their credit and their reputations on the line to guarantee an additional thirty-one-million-dollar loan from Equitable Life Assurance Society . . . a loan that will take thirty years to pay off.

Nor is it out of order to mention the fact that we and the football Cardinals committed ourselves for thirty-year leases.

Incidentally, not one of the men, or the organizations, who put up the twenty million dollars will ever live to see a single penny of that money returned to them.

It does say one helluva lot for what those businessmen think about the future of professional sports in our town . . . and we don't propose to let them down.

Gentlemen, in a few days I'm going to celebrate my seventieth birthday. I can assure you I didn't need a new ball park. But I can also assure you that baseball did very much need a new ball park.

As a matter of fact, in some other cities, where they delayed building new ball parks, attendance has dropped off seriously.

In some cities, the taxpayers put up the millions necessary to build a park through bond issues. In St. Louis, however, business and labor joined hands to provide the money and the Stadium.

Times have changed in just a very few years, and people won't go and pay their money where they don't have all the modern conveniences, such as we now have at new Busch Stadium.

And there is still another factor. Many professional sports now overlap the baseball season very seriously and very strongly for the entertainment dollar.

We no longer have a monopoly. We no longer are the only game in town. People paid to watch professional basketball up to a few months ago in St. Louis.

People are now turning out in droves to watch professional ice hockey.

And, millions of people are packing the football stadiums all over the country.

And, millions more are listening and watching all of these sports on radio and television . . . and right during the baseball season. I don't think I have to remind you of this competition.

But, I wonder if we are putting them all in focus these days.

If you don't already know it, I can tell you now—from the letters, phone calls, and conversations we've had recently—that fans are no longer as sure as they were before about their high regard for the game and the players.

Sports authorities all over the country are writing and talking about it, almost all the time, it seems.

Let's take a good look at the past winter ourselves. What do we see?

We almost didn't have any season at all.

Some of our players who ought to be in top condition reported late for spring training.

Baseball's union representatives made all kinds of derogatory statements about the owners. We suddenly seemed to be your greatest enemies.

Your representatives threw down all kinds of challenges, threats and ultimatums.

Some players made statements over radio and television, and to newspapermen, in which they, too, reflected upon the owners.

Some of them said that the real problem was that the owners wanted to keep *all* the radio and television money for themselves, even when they must have known that was far removed from the facts.

Now, let me make myself very clear. I am not arguing with your right or the right of your representatives to say and do whatever they believe serves yours or their best interests.

What I am saying—loud and clear—is that I think we ought to give consideration . . . all of us, the owners, the players and their representatives . . . to what we have to gain and what we have to lose by these tactics.

And . . . let me get something else straight . . . I am not suggesting that you should not have a union, or union representatives. That's up to you.

We live in a free country, and you are entitled to whatever kind of representation you want.

As a matter of record, our Company has negotiated with dozens of unions for almost a hundred years . . . and for the last twenty-five years Dick Meyer has been our chief negotiator. I think we know something about union negotiations.

As players, you are entitled to get the best deal you can, and I believe you have. We have the biggest payroll for players in the entire history of baseball. Nor am I suggesting that you should not even have individual business manager or even press agents. This is your privilege.

I am saying, though, we are beginning to lose sight of who really has to pay the ultimate bill for your salary and your pension . . . namely, the fan. And when we do that, I think we do have a problem. It's a problem which should be of mutual concern to all of us.

That is why I ought to talk to you very frankly about this situation this morning.

Believe me, it wasn't easy for most owners to agree not to answer back some of the allegations, charges, ultimatums, and challenges thrown down to us during the past months. But, in the main, we didn't engage in this kind of inter-quarreling because we didn't think it would help baseball or the players.

In any case, you now have the most liberal pension plan to be found anywhere, in any business, in any profession, or in any sport in the whole world.

As a group, your salaries are higher than they have ever been at any time.

It has actually reached the stage now where a young man who has any talent at all for baseball would do well to look into it as a serious profession because of the good pay and the lifetime security which it gives him in his early stage of life. And it only takes a relatively few years to make it.

It used to be that some parents looked down their noses at the thought of their sons going into professional baseball.

Today, that's all changed. Making the grade in the major leagues is just about the most productive thing that could happen to any young man.

In addition to being well paid during his baseball days, there are even greater opportunities for a player to make lasting and profitable business connections mostly because they played major league baseball.

Many of you have already done that. Stan Musial, Lou Brock, Curt Flood, Tim McCarver, Roger Maris and many others are already in that category. And you know it.

True, you deserve to be well paid in accordance with your playing ability. But I must call your attention to the fact of life that you take few, if any, of the great risks involved.

I know you may think I am lecturing to you. And some of you will be very cynical about what I have said. I must tell you that it's all right with me.

I do believe, however, that as the president of a major league baseball team, with the highest salary total in all the history of baseball, I have a right to talk to you and to talk to you as men . . . frankly straight-from-the-shoulder.

Certainly, some of you have been talking to me through the press. I don't mind it at all.

I do believe I have an obligation to remind you that this year—instead of talking baseball all during the off-season—most fans have had a steady diet of strike talk and dollar signs.

I hope that is all behind us now. It has to be behind us. Too many fans are saying our players are getting fat . . . that they now only think of money . . . and less of the game itself. And it's the game they love and have enjoyed and paid for all these years.

Fans are telling us now that if we intend to raise prices to pay for the high salaries and so on and on, they will stop coming to the games, they will not watch and will not listen. They say they can do other things with their time and with their money.

It doesn't take a crystal ball, gentlemen, to realize that with so many fans being so aware of the big payrolls in baseball, they will become more and more critical of all of us.

I hope that many millions of fans will retain their loyalty to baseball. We are going to do everything we can do to make sure they do.

But I know you are bound to have some bad days.

I know you are bound to lose some ball games.

I know you are bound to make some errors and sometimes the ball just won't bounce the way you think it should.

But, you can bet on one thing . . . the fans will be looking at you this year more critically than ever before to watch how you perform and see whether or not you are really giving everything you have.

I am not asking you to do anything for me.

I am not going to talk about such corny things as "hustle." That's supposed to be old-fashioned.

But, if we don't have the right attitudes, if we don't give everything we have to those who pay their way into the park, then you can be sure they'll know it and we'll know it.

There are just a few final words I'd like to add.

They are not accusations. They are statements based upon what so many people have written to us and have told us about personally.

I can only share them with you. It's up to each of you to accept or to reject them.

I urge you to watch your attitudes.

I plead with you not to kill the enthusiasm of the fans and the kids for whom you have become such idols.

They are the ones who make you popular.

They are the ones who make your salary and pension possible.

We are told that many ball players have begun to ignore the fans.

We are told that too many ball players are refusing to sign autographs.

We are told that some of the ball players fail to show up for scheduled appointments.

We are told that some ball players push kids aside when they try to take their pictures.

We remember, a few years ago, when player representatives told us they would refuse to be interviewed unless they were paid extra for it.

Gentlemen, all I want to say is . . . that when media people lose interest—when they stop asking you for interviews—when kids don't want your autographs—when they stop trying to take your picture . . . then we better all begin to worry.

We better concern ourselves about the future of the game that has meant so much to so many of us.

That's about it. I have mentioned the fact that I will be seventy years old in a few days. But I don't want anyone in the meeting—or any place else—to think for one minute that I have lost any of my will to win.

I don't like to lose now any more than I did fifty years ago.

I don't believe you have lost your desire or your will to win either.

We are about to begin a new season.

Let's show the world that we are the real champions.

Let's get off to a good start—and carry it all through the season.

Personally, I don't react well to ultimatums. I don't mind negotiations—that's how we get together—but ultimatums rub me the wrong way, and I think ultimatums rub the fans the wrong way.

This is no "pep" talk. I have not tried to bawl you out. But . . . I have tried to point out baseball is at a serious point in its history.

I don't know what the future will bring.

I do believe we can shape and influence that future.

If you are counting on security at age fifty—or sixty-five—then you have an obligation to help make the people who love this game—who pay to see it played—who listen to it day after day—enjoy watching and listening to it.

Last year a lot of people were saying that you were an accident—and that you couldn't repeat again. Many are saying the same things again this year.

Only you can prove whether they are right or wrong.

I wish you all the very best of success and sincerely hope that baseball has made possible a great future and personal security for you and your families.

Thank you and good luck.